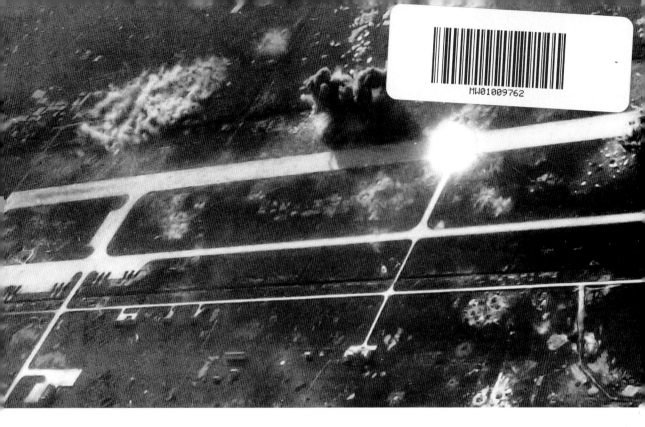

AIR CAMPAIGN

ROLLING THUNDER
1965–68

Johnson's air war over Vietnam

RICHARD P. HALLION | ILLUSTRATED BY ADAM TOOBY

Osprey Publishing
c/o Bloomsbury Publishing Plc
PO Box 883, Oxford, OX1 9PL, UK
Or
c/o Bloomsbury Publishing Inc.
1385 Broadway, 5th Floor, New York, NY 10018, USA
E-mail: info@ospreypublishing.com

www.ospreypublishing.com

OSPREY is a trademark of Osprey Publishing Ltd, a division of Bloomsbury Publishing Plc.

First published in Great Britain in 2018

A CIP catalog record for this book is available from the British Library.

ISBN: PB: 9781472823205
ePub: 9781472823212
ePDF: 9781472823182
XML 9781472823199

18 19 20 21 22   10 9 8 7 6 5 4 3 2 1

Index by Angela Hall
Typeset in Adobe Garamond Pro, Futura Std, Sabon and Akzidenz-Grotesk Condensed
Cartography and command diagrams by bounford.com
Formation and 3D diagrams by Adam Tooby
3D BEVs by The Black Spot
Page layouts by PDQ Digital Media Solutions, Bungay, UK
Printed in China through World Print Ltd.

Front Cover: Art by Adam Tooby © Osprey Publishing
Back Cover: Photo courtesy NHHC

Osprey Publishing supports the Woodland Trust, the UK's leading woodland conservation charity. Between 2014 and 2018 our donations are being spent on their Centenary Woods project in the UK.

To find out more about our authors and books visit www.ospreypublishing.com. Here you will find extracts, author interviews, details of forthcoming events and the option to sign up for our newsletter.

Image credits:
DoD: Department of Defense
JFKL: John F. Kennedy Presidential Library
LBJL: Lyndon B. Johnson Presidential Library
LC: Library of Congress
NARA: National Archives and Records Administration
NHHC: Naval History and Heritage Command
NMUSAF: National Museum of the US Air Force
NWC: Naval Weapons Center China Lake
USAF: US Air Force
USMC: US Marine Corps

Title page image:
A bomb explodes on Phuc Yen air base during the first raid on October 24, 1967. (NMUSAF)

CONTENTS

INTRODUCTION

President Lyndon Johnson (center) and Secretary of Defense Robert McNamara (to Johnson's left) meeting with senior staff to discuss Vietnam, July 22, 1965, two days before the first loss of an American aircraft to a Soviet Vympel S-75 Dvina (NATO SA-2 Guideline) surface-to-air missile (SAM). (LBJL)

The phrase "Vietnam War" is a convenient shorthand for what was in reality a series of interlinked conflicts. In the early 1960s, growing insurgencies in Laos and South Vietnam triggered a steadily expanding US commitment to Southeast Asia (SEA) that soon erupted into a full-blown war. Fighting raged over South Vietnam, Laos, Cambodia, and into Thailand. The supporters of South Vietnam (the Republic of Vietnam, or RVN) included the United States, Australia, Canada, Britain, the Republic of China (ROC, now Taiwan), South Korea (the Republic of Korea, ROK), Japan, Malaysia, New Zealand, the Philippines, Spain, Thailand, and West Germany. North Korea (the Democratic People's Republic of Korea, DPRK), the People's Republic of China (PRC), the Soviet Union (USSR), Czechoslovakia, Cuba, East Germany, Hungary, Poland, and Romania supported North Vietnam (the Democratic Republic of Vietnam, or DRV) and aided Communist insurgents in South Vietnam, Laos, and Cambodia.

US participation lasted 5,182 days: February 28, 1961 through May 7, 1975, over 14 years of continuous conflict – making it America's longest 20th-century conflict, exceeded only by the 19th century's Native American wars, and by the unbroken succession of counter-terrorism operations undertaken since September 11, 2001. To those who fought in Vietnam, whether on land, sea or in the air, the war highlighted serious doctrinal, training, force-structure, and technological deficiencies in America's military machine. The war's grim calculus of loss, disappointment, and failure has furnished fodder for military staff colleges and academies, and a plethora of postwar studies.

Just as there was no single "Vietnam war," there was no single "Vietnam air war." Rather, South Vietnam, the United States, and their allies operated covert air missions over Laos and Cambodia; a complex "in-country" air war across South Vietnam of reconnaissance, aerial defoliation, air transport, helicopter-based troop-insertion and aerial fire-support attacks, fixed-wing battlefield air interdiction (BAI) and close air support (CAS); a littoral maritime and riverine air support war; and an on-and-off-and-on-again air war over North Vietnam.

Operation *Rolling Thunder* (1965–68) is at once both Vietnam's most controversial air campaign and also the most controversial air campaign in all of American 20th-century air power history, even including the early days of daylight bombing against Nazi Germany in 1942–43. Its troubled record has subsequently shaped the theory and practice of American air war – influencing its doctrine, training, planning, and operational execution – as evidenced by subsequent American air campaigns.

In 1965, when *Rolling Thunder* commenced, South Vietnam faced collapse. A military coup – supported by the United States – against President Ngo Dình Diem in early November 1963 had led to his death and created political chaos. Over the next 15 months, DRV assistance to South Vietnamese and Laotian insurgents increased dramatically, and units of the People's Army of Vietnam (PAVN) crossed into Laos and the South. After sporadic retaliatory air strikes following several Viet Cong and North Vietnamese actions against American and South Vietnamese forces and facilities – the Tonkin Gulf incident (August 1964), and attacks on Bien Hoa air base (November 1964), a Saigon hotel (December 1964); the Pleiku airfield and support base (February 1965), and a Quy Nhon enlisted men's billet (February 1965) – failed to curb rising Viet Cong violence in the South, President Johnson and his senior defense team launched *Rolling Thunder*.

At its core, *Rolling Thunder* reflected the frustration and increasing alarm of the White House and the Pentagon as South Vietnam and Laos rapidly unraveled. It sought to influence the DRV's leadership to cease their support of Viet Cong guerrillas in South Vietnam and Pathet Lao insurgents in Laos. Thus, though ostensibly separate from the day-to-day air support war already run over South Vietnam (including reconnaissance and trail interdiction missions over northern and southern Laos and Cambodia), *Rolling Thunder*'s air strikes over the North were intended to influence the war's political–military outcome in the South.

As executed, *Rolling Thunder* was more a series of individual operations conducted in fits and starts than a coherent air campaign, and it suffered accordingly. An exceptional degree of "out of theater" civilian input characterized its planning, oversight, and execution. Various Johnson administration political figures – all, as a group, both untrained and inexperienced in military strategy, operational art, and tactics, particularly air warfare – overturned previous national security practice by consolidating direct control of target selection and approval at the Executive Branch (e.g. Presidential and Executive Agency senior staff) level, based on various inputs they received from US Pacific Command (Military Assistance Command Vietnam, MACV; the US Air Force's Pacific Air Forces, USAF PACAF; and the US Navy's Pacific Fleet, USN PACFLT), and the national intelligence apparatus (the Central Intelligence Agency, CIA; the National Security Agency, NSA; and service military intelligence components). Indeed, the control of targeting largely occurred within the West Wing of the White House itself. Principal participants included President Lyndon Johnson and his senior staff, particularly National Security Advisor McGeorge Bundy, Secretary of State Dean Rusk, and Secretary of Defense Robert McNamara.

From the outset America's uniformed military leadership – from the Joint Chiefs of Staff (JCS) down through regional and theater commanders – expressed reservations about the scope and intent of *Rolling Thunder*, as did the operational commanders and airmen under their command who were tasked with its execution. Though *Rolling Thunder* took North Vietnam's leaders by surprise, very quickly DRV air defenders adapted, learning how to confront American airmen with a mix of fighters, surface-to-air missiles (SAMs) and antiaircraft fire, assisted as well by sapper attacks directed against American air bases in South Vietnam and Thailand. Abroad, *Rolling Thunder* accelerated an international antiwar protest movement, ultimately triggering Lyndon Johnson's decision not to run for re-election in 1968. In doing this, it changed the course of the war, which continued off-and-on until North Vietnam overran South Vietnam in April 1975.

CHRONOLOGY

1964

August 2–5 DRV naval attack on USS *Maddox* triggers *Pierce Arrow.*

August Joint Chiefs of Staff (JCS) identify 94 key DRV targets.

October Undersecretary of State George Ball reveals Johnson and senior officials are contemplating DRV air attacks.

November 1 Bien Hoa air base attack.

December 24 Saigon Brinks Hotel bombing.

1965

February 7–8 Pleiku attack triggers *Flaming Dart.*

February 9–11 Quy Nhon quarters attack triggers *Flaming Dart II.*

February 13 President Johnson approves *Rolling Thunder.*

March 2 *Rolling Thunder V*, first actual strike.

March 6 President Johnson tells Senator Richard Russell "There ain't no daylight in Vietnam," and Russell replies "There's no end to the road."

March 8–10 Ambassador Maxwell Taylor criticizes "timid" attacks to McNamara and JCS Chairman Wheeler, calling them "a few isolated thunderclaps."

March 14–15 *Rolling Thunder VI* by USAF–USN–VNAF; USN first strike on March 15.

March 26–April 1 *Rolling Thunder VIII*, targets radar sites, barracks, and road recce.

March 29 Viet Cong bomb US Embassy in Saigon.

April 3–4 VPAF MiG-17s enter combat, damage F-8E on 3rd, shoot down two F-105Ds on 4th.

April 5 First S-75 (NATO SA-2 Guideline) SAM site discovered.

April 9 USN F-4Bs tangle with Chinese J-5 (MiG-17) fighters off Hainan Island, losing one aircraft but claiming a J-5.

April 2–29 *Rolling Thunder IX–XII*, emphasizes interdiction.

April 20 At Honolulu conference, McNamara criticizes road recce effort, stresses focused air attacks against logistics targets near Demilitarized Zone.

April 28 CIA Director John McCone resigns over *Rolling Thunder.*

May 6 McNamara rejects JCS recommendation to attack SAM sites.

May 13–18 Bombing pause.

June 11–17 *Rolling Thunder XVIII* extends operations above 20 degrees North.

June 15 McNamara again rejects SAM attacks fearing provoking USSR.

June 17 First confirmed shootdown of VPAF MiG-17, by USN F-4B.

June 25–July 1 *Rolling Thunder XX*, strikes Lines of Communications (LOCs).

Early July First S-75 Dvina (SA-2 Guideline) site is operational.

July 1 Undersecretary of State Ball recommends negotiating end to war.

July 10 First shootdown of VPAF MiG-17 by USAF F-4C.

July 24 USAF F-4C downed by SA-2, first Southeast Asia SAM loss.

July 28 First USAF counter-SAM strike costs six aircraft.

August 13 First USN counter-SAM strike costs five aircraft.

September 2 JCS JCSM-670-65 recommends expanding *Rolling Thunder*; is rejected.

December 10 US Pacific Command (PACOM) divides North Vietnam into six "Route Packages."

December 22 First destruction of SA-2 site by Wild Weasel F-100F.

December 24–January 31, 1966 Bombing pause.

1966
January MiG-21F-13 Fishbed enters VPAF service.

Late March McNamara finally recommends bombing petroleum–oil–lubricants (POL); LBJ defers three months.

April 12 SAC B-52s strike Mu Gia Pass, first B-52 strike in North Vietnam.

May 6 Administration advisor Walt Rostow recommends a POL campaign.

June 29 Onset of *Rolling Thunder* Hanoi–Haiphong POL campaign, with air strikes by the 355th and 388th Tactical Fighter Wings (TFWs), *Constellation*'s CVW-9, and *Ranger*'s CVW-14.

July 8 Honolulu conference reveals Johnson has designated DRV POL as *Rolling Thunder*'s top targeting priority.

July 24 CINCPAC Admiral Ulysses S. G. Sharp urges attacking Phuc Yen and Kép airfields to expedite POL campaign.

August 20 Admiral Sharp recommends against reducing, pausing, or halting *Rolling Thunder*.

August 29 Jasons advisory group recommends physical barrier across the Ho Chi Minh Trail; McNamara subsequently concurs.

October 23–25 Manila conference; General William Westmoreland, MACV, opposes curtailing *Rolling Thunder*.

November 4 JCS JCSM 7-2-66 recommends continuing *Rolling Thunder*.

December 24–26 Bombing pause: Christmas truce.

December 31–January 1, 1967 Bombing pause: New Year's truce.

1967
January 2 Led by Colonel Robin Olds, 8th TFW "Wolfpack" executes Operation *Bolo*, downing seven MiG-21s in 12 minutes.

January 18 Sharp recommends targeting electrical power, industry, transportation, logistics, POL, and ports.

February 22 Johnson approves mining waterways and attacking Thai Nguyen iron and steel complex.

February 27 First waterway mining.

March 10 First Thai Nguyen raid.

March 20–21 Guam conference approves B-52 Thailand basing.

March 24 ADF-VPAF reorganizes regional air defense commands.

April 1 Beginning of *Rolling Thunder* railroad and highway interdiction effort.

April 8 *Rolling Thunder LV* strikes Hanoi power and industry.

April 27 Westmoreland tells Johnson he is "dismayed" at prospect of halting *Rolling Thunder*.

May 12 CIA concludes *Rolling Thunder* has not significantly eroded DRV morale or capabilities.

May 19 VA-212 Walleye attack on Hanoi thermal power plant.

May 20–October 17 JCS advocates attacking airfields, ports, LOCs, and further mining.

August 9–25 Stennis Hearings bitterly criticize McNamara's conduct of *Rolling Thunder*.

August 11 355th TFW drops Doumer Bridge.

October 2 In a private meeting, Colonel Robin Olds advises Lyndon Johnson to "destroy [DRV's] ability to fight."

October 21 50,000 war protestors march on Pentagon.

October 24 First Phuc Yen raid.

November 28 McNamara resigns.

December 22 Pope Paul VI calls for an end to bombing.

December 24–25 Christmas truce.

December 31– January 1, 1968 New Year's truce.

1968
January 2 MACV declares *Rolling Thunder* "indispensable" for morale.

January 21 Siege of Khe Sanh opens.

January 23 North Korean seizure of the USS *Pueblo* (AGER-2).

January 29 Tet truce.

January 31 DRV launches Tet offensive.

February 29 Last *Rolling Thunder* SAM loss.

March 31 Johnson announces bombing restrictions and not seeking re-election.

April 1 US ends "all offensive air efforts north of 20 degrees North latitude."

April 3 *Rolling Thunder* restricted to Route Packs I, II, and III.

May 23 MiG-21 destroyed by Talos fired by USS *Long Beach.*

July General Creighton Abrams succeeds Westmoreland at MACV.

August Seventh Air Force begins "Vietnamization" of air war.

October 31 *Rolling Thunder* ends.

November 1 President Johnson halts all bombing of North except "protective reaction" in defense of reconnaissance missions.

North American F-100D Super Sabre (SN 56-3415) firing 2.75in podded Folding Fin Aerial Rockets (FFARs) against the Viet Cong, 1967. The pod-fired 2.75in FFAR was wildly inaccurate, individual rockets typically dispersing widely immediately after launch, sometimes colliding and endangering the aircraft or helicopter that launched them. (NMUSAF)

ATTACKERS' CAPABILITIES
US Cold War air power

In August 1945, the age of atomic warfare dawned with the dropping of atomic bombs on Hiroshima and Nagasaki. In June 1948, an ultimately unsuccessful Soviet blockade of Berlin signaled the onset of the Cold War. Over 1949, the Soviet Union tightened its grip on Eastern Europe and detonated its first atomic bomb; China fell to Mao Zedong; and insurgencies erupted in Greece, Malaya, and Indochina. In June 1950, North Korean troops invaded South Korea, subsequently saved through a combination of dogged resistance and the United Nations coalition's total air, materiel, and logistical superiority.

Though Western air power analysts studied Korea and other limited war contingencies, soon conventional-style war would largely drop from American and European public and policy consciousness, replaced by growing fears of global nuclear war. In 1953, the United States Air Force had issued Air Force Manual 1-2 (AFM 1-2), which reaffirmed the central role of strategic bombing in attacking an enemy's heartland, and emphasized nuclear attack in future wars. Between then and 1961, President Dwight D. Eisenhower's administration emphasized nuclear deterrence through a strategy of "massive retaliation." Over Eisenhower's Presidency, the US Air Force and US Navy acquired sophisticated nuclear-armed fighters, interceptors, bombers, and missiles; and the US Army deployed atomic cannon and ballistic and surface-to-air missiles. The Soviet bomber threat – not as profound as initially thought – drove development of an air defense network of radars, specialized jet interceptors, and both surface-to-air and air-to-air missiles, some with atomic warheads. Air power was NATO's linchpin, with conventional ground forces effectively a "trip-wire" to trigger an overwhelming USAF and Royal Air Force (RAF) nuclear response, assisted by attack aircraft from US Navy and Royal Navy (RN) carrier strike forces and, later, from Polaris-launching submarines operating deep at sea.

In February 1965, the United States Air Force, Navy, and Marine Corps possessed over 23,500 aircraft. Of these, 371 fighters, bombers, and attack aircraft were available for *Rolling Thunder*: 166 of the Pacific Air Force's 2nd Air Division, based in South Vietnam and

The eight-engine Boeing B-52 Stratofortress exemplified America's global nuclear reach; here is a late production B-52H (SN 60-0006) during flight testing. (USAF)

In the mid-1960s missiles and guided weapons of all types were promising but troublesome. The early Sparrow proved frustratingly disappointing, F-4 crews complaining of how often it either "broke lock" or "went stupid" immediately after launch. The early heat-seeking AIM-9B could lose a MiG against the sun, and had difficulty tracking and closing on a hard-maneuvering fighter. This photo shows Raytheon AIM-7E Sparrow air-to-air missiles being readied for loading on Air Force F-4C Phantom IIs, Da Nang, South Vietnam, February 1967. (NMUSAF)

Thailand, and 205 naval aircraft from Task Force 77 (TF-77) in the South China Sea.

Headquartered at Tan Son Nhut air base in South Vietnam and commanded by Major General Joseph H. Moore Jr, the 2nd Air Division dated to World War II. So, too, did Rear Admiral Henry L. Miller's Task Force 77, the carrier striking force of the US Seventh Fleet. Highly regarded by superiors and subordinates alike, both Moore and Miller had fought with distinction as young officers in World War II. Moore shot down two Mitsubishi A6M Type 0 "Zeros" over the Philippines before escaping to Australia. Miller taught Doolittle's Tokyo raiders how to fly their B-25s off the USS *Hornet* (CV-8), then commanded Carrier Air Groups on the USS *Princeton* (CVL-23) and USS *Hancock* (CV-19). Moore's and Miller's airmen were also combat-proven, having flown Laotian reconnaissance and some air strikes, particularly after North Vietnamese MTBs attacked the USS *Maddox* (DD-731) on August 2, 1964 in the Tonkin Gulf.

Douglas A-4C Skyhawk (BuNo 147781) drops a Martin AGM-62 Walleye at the Naval Weapons Center, China Lake, California. The Martin AGM-62 Walleye TV-guided glide bomb had too small a warhead – just 825lb – to seriously damage a "hardened" target, and though the pilot could lock the bomb's camera onto a target and immediately take evasive action after dropping it, if the target did not stand out sufficiently from its surrounding background, the Walleye could miss. (NWC)

Responding to Viet Cong and DRV aggression, the Air Force had deployed 54 North American F-100D Super Sabres and 36 Republic F-105D Thunderchiefs; and 28 Martin B-57B Canberras. These joined 48 Douglas A-1E Skyraider propeller-driven attack aircraft operated by Air Force Air Commandos to support South Vietnam's army. (Ten Convair F-102A Delta Dagger interceptors deployed for air base defense but did not count as offensive assets; neither did armed *Farm Gate* North American T-28 trainers then in-country.) Embarked on the *Ranger* (CVA-61), *Coral Sea* (CVA-43), and *Hancock* (CVA-19) were 205 fighter and attack aircraft: 36 McDonnell F-4B Phantom IIs; 36 Vought F-8D/E Crusader fighters; 15 Douglas A-3B Skywarrior heavy attack aircraft; 82 Douglas A-4C/E Skyhawk light attack aircraft; and 36 Douglas A-1H/J Skyraiders. TF-77's air wings also had detachments of reconnaissance, tanker, and electronic warfare aircraft, and search and rescue helicopters.

PRINCIPAL LAND-BASED AND NAVAL STRIKE AIRCRAFT AT THE ONSET OF ROLLING THUNDER					
Naval-Marine Aircraft					
Type	Speed[1] (kts & Mach)	Radius[2]	Cannon(s)	Air-to-Air Missiles	Air-Ground Weapons[3]
A-1H	300kt; Mach 0.48	565nm	4× 20mm	No	8,000lb
A-3B	530kt; Mach 0.83	912nm	no	no	12,000lb
A-4E	585kt; Mach 0.89	504nm	2× 20mm	no	8,200lb
F-4B	1,290kt; Mach 2.25	563nm	no[4]	4–6 AIM-7, 2–4 AIM-9	16,000lb
F-8E	973kt; Mach 1.70	394nm	4× 20mm	4× AIM-9	6,000lb
US Air Force Aircraft					
Type	Speed[1]	Radius[2]	Cannon	Air-to-Air Guided	Air-Ground Weapons[3]
A-1E	270kt; Mach 0.44	522nm	4× 20mm	no	8,000lb
B-57B	520kt; Mach 0.79	824nm	4× 20mm	no	6,000lb
F-100D	740kt; Mach 1.30	311nm	4× 20mm	2–4 AIM-9	4,500lb
F-105D	1,192kt; Mach 2.08	506nm	1× 20mm M-61	2–4 AIM-9	12,000lb
Notes					
1 Figures are for a "clean" airplane at its best altitude. In practice, drag of pylons and weapons greatly reduced speed. Seeming inconsistencies in Mach number for close or identical kts reflect speed of sound variation with altitude. 2 In practice, all strike aircraft (excepting the A-1) could (and did) air refuel during combat sorties. 3 Such as bombs, bomblet dispensers, napalm tanks, rockets, rocket pods, guided missiles, and mines. 4 The F-4 lacked cannon, in the foolish expectation that all it needed were air-to-air missiles; in 1969 the USAF F-4E introduced an integral 20mm M-61 in a redesigned nose; until the introduction of the F-4E, some USAF Phantoms occasionally carried a M61 gun pod on the centerline stores station, though it added drag and had poor accuracy.					

By summer 1968, the Air Force had expanded to 1,337 fighter and attack aircraft in theater: 737 in Vietnam, at Bien Hoa, Cam Ranh, Da Nang, Phan Rang, Phu Cat, Tan Son Nhut and Tuy Hoa; and 600 in Thailand, at Korat, Nakhon Phanom, Takhli, Ubon, Udorn, and U-Tapao. The Navy had 16 attack carriers: *Ticonderoga* (CVA-14), *Hancock* (CVA-19), *Bon Homme Richard* (CVA-31), *Shangri-La* (CVA-38), *Oriskany* (CVA-34), *Midway* (CVA-41), *Franklin D. Roosevelt* (CVA-42), *Coral Sea* (CVA-43), *Forrestal* (CVA-59), *Saratoga* (CVA-60), *Ranger* (CVA-61), *Independence* (CVA-62); *Enterprise* (CVAN-65), *Kitty Hawk* (CVA-63), *Constellation* (CVA-64), and *America* (CVA-66). Given the Navy's global responsibilities, having just 16 taxed its ability to maintain three or four at sea with TF-77, with three others in port at Yokosuka, Hong Kong, and Cubi Point. Carrier Air Wings (CVWs) varied from 70 to over 100 aircraft, depending on the vessel. Patrol, counterinsurgency, and support squadrons operated from shore and, in the case of seaplanes, from moored tenders.

A Martin AGM-12B Bullpup A launched from a VP-23 Lockheed P-3B Orion. The rocket-boosted command-guided AGM-12 Bullpup had an even smaller 250lb warhead and added another deficiency: it required the pilot to steer it by watching a flare at the rear of the missile and then using a small joystick to guide it into its target. But since the Bullpup had at best a range between 10 and 12 miles, this meant following the missile on a straight and predictable flight path that brought the launch airplane ever closer to the target – and ever closer to its antiaircraft defenses. (NHHC)

As the DRV's strengthened its defenses, signals intelligence and electronic warfare (SIGINT-EW) assumed crucial significance. Electronic warfare and SAM-killers such as the A-6B, EA-1F, EA-3B, EA-6A, EF-10B, EB-66B/C/E, EKA-3B, and F-100F and F-105F Wild Weasel deployed to Thailand, South Vietnam, or the Fleet. USAF, USN, USMC, and CIA reconnaissance aircraft collected intelligence, vitally influencing decision-making and operations. These included Boeing RB-47H and RC-135Ms, Lockheed U-2s, A-12 and SR-71 Blackbirds, EC-121 Constellations, and EC-130 Hercules; McDonnell RF-101 Voodoos and RF-4B/C Phantom IIs; Vought RF-8A/G Crusaders; North American RA-5C Vigilantes; and Lockheed DC-130 Hercules air-launching Ryan 147 Firebee drones.

Aircraft, weapons, and ordnance

Rolling Thunder's principal attackers were the tri-service Navy–Marine–USAF F-4 Phantom II; the Navy–Marine F-8 Crusader, A-4 Skyhawk, and A-6 Intruder; and the Air Force F-105 Thunderchief. All had strengths and weaknesses reflecting doctrine, perceived operational needs, and the state of aviation design technology at mid-century.

The two-place twin-engine Mach 2-plus McDonnell F-4 Phantom II (formerly F4H prior to implementation of the McNamara-mandated 1962 redesignation scheme for all military aircraft) was then the world's most powerful and advanced fighter. It had an excellent radar, carried a variety of air-to-air and air-to-surface weapons, and had great power enabling it to fight in the vertical plane. Still, it had several weaknesses: it lacked any cannon (a deficiency rectified with the introduction of the M61 20mm Vulcan-armed F-4E in late 1968); was out-turned by the MiG-17 and (at lower speeds) by the MiG-21; lacked good rear visibility; and its J79 engines generated a highly visible sooty trail, increasing its detectability.

The Vought F-8 (formerly F8U) Crusader proved a formidable dogfighter, armed with Sidewinders and four 20mm cannon, though it, too, lacked good visibility aft. Its strengths were good high-speed acceleration, roll, and turn rates, and its overall performance closely matched the MiG-21F-13 (including comparable fuel usage), though with better controllability and much faster low-altitude limitations. Like other early swept-wing supersonic fighters such as the F-100 and F-105, it was unforgiving of pilot error, and, again like the F-105, it had a hydraulic-boosted flight control system notoriously vulnerable to shrapnel, with frequently catastrophic results.

The single- or-two-seat Republic F-105 Thunderchief was a supersonic low-level NATO strike fighter designed to carry a nuclear bomb in an internal bomb bay. In Vietnam it flew as a transonic level-and-dive bomber (and SAM-hunter) carrying performance-robbing external bombs, rockets, and missiles. Once freed of its weapons, the "Thud's" sleek shape and powerful J75 engine ensured an astonishingly high egress speed, but even minor hits to its hydraulic system often spelled disaster. "Thuds" flew 75 percent of Air Force *Rolling Thunder* attack missions, becoming the service's iconic airplane.

LAND-BASED AND NAVAL STRIKE AIRCRAFT AS ROLLING THUNDER MATURED

Naval–Marine Aircraft

Type	Speed[1] (kts & Mach)	Radius[2]	Cannon(s)	Air-to-Air Missiles	Air-Ground Weapons[3]
A-1J	300kts; Mach 0.48	565nm	4× 20mm	no	8,000lb
A-3B	530kts; Mach 0.83	912nm	no	no	12,000lb
A-4F	590kts; Mach 0.90	539nm	2× 20mm	no	8,200lb
A-6A	561kts; Mach 0.85	585nm	no	4× AIM-9	15,000lb
A-7A	595kts; Mach 0.90	569nm	2× 20mm	2× AIM-9	8,000lb
EA-1F	250kts; Mach 0.40	500nm	4× 20mm	no	EW/ECM suite only
EA-3B	530kts; Mach 0.83	912nm	no	no	EW/ECM suite only
EA-6A[4]	489kts; Mach 0.83	516nm	no	no	EW/ECM suite only
EF-10B	428kts; Mach 0.75	497nm	4× 20mm	no	EW/ECM suite only
F-4J	1,290kts; Mach 2.25	563nm	no	4–6 AIM-7, 2–4 AIM-9	16,000lb.
F-8E	973kts; Mach 1.70	394nm	4× 20mm	4× AIM-9	6,000lb.

US Air Force Aircraft

Type	Speed[1]	Radius[2]	Cannon	Air-to-Air Guided	Air-Ground Weapons[3]
A-1E	270kts; Mach 0.44	522nm	4× 20mm	no	8,000lb
EB-66C	533kts; Mach 0.83	947nm	no	no	EW/ECM suite only
F-4D	1,290kts; Mach 2.25	563nm	no[5]	4–6 AIM-7, 2–4 AIM-9[6]	16,000lb
F-100D	740kts; Mach 1.30	311nm	4× 20mm	2–4 AIM-9	4,500lb
F-100F[7]	740kts; Mach 1.30	311nm	2× 20mm	2–4 AIM-9	4,500lb
F-104C	1,347kts; Mach 2.35	306nm	1× 20mm M-61	2–4 AIM-9	1,500lb
F-105D	1,192kts; Mach 2.08	506nm	1× 20mm M61	2–4 AIM-9	12,000lb
F-105F[8]	1,169kts; Mach 2.04	500nm	1× 20mm M61	1–2 AIM-9	12,000lb
F-111A[9]	1,260kts; Mach 2.20	540nm	1× 20mm M61	4–6 AIM-9[10]	8,000lb

Notes

1 Figures are for a "clean" airplane at its best altitude. In practice, drag of pylons and weapons greatly reduced speed. Seeming inconsistencies in Mach number for close or identical kts reflect speed of sound variation with altitude.
2 In practice, all strike aircraft (excepting the A-1 and EF-10B) could (and did) air refuel during combat sorties.
3 Such as bombs, bomblet dispensers, napalm tanks, rockets, rocket pods, guided missiles, and mines.
4 Used for electronic combat, typically jamming and for strike force protection; USMC only operator.
5 Pending introduction of the M61 20mm in the F-4E in 1968, USAF F-4C and F-4D Phantoms occasionally carried a M61 gun pod on the centerline stores station, though it added drag and had relatively poor accuracy.
6 The F-4D variant initially employed the AIM-4 Falcon, which proved so disappointing in combat that F-4Ds were quickly modified to employ the AIM-9.
7 Two-place F-100s primarily employed as "fast-FAC" Misty Forward Air Controllers in Route Pack I, with drop tanks and marking rockets; some F-100Fs with EW/ECM were used with mixed results as anti-SAM Wild Weasels in December 1965–July 1966, pending combat debut of first F-105F Wild Weasels.
8 Two-place F-105 Wild Weasel SAM-killers fitted with anti-SAM EW, employing GP bombs, cluster bombs, unguided rockets, and AGM-45 (and later AGM-78) anti-radar missiles (ARMs).
9 Six F-111As sent on Combat Lancer Operational Test and Evaluation (OT&E) trials, Takhli RTAB, Spring 1968.
10 The F-111A rarely carried any AAMs, serving as a night low-level terrain-following attacker.

Airmen in *Rolling Thunder* flew the Navy-Marine F-4B, F-4J, and RF-4B, and their Air Force equivalents, the F-4C, F-4D, and RF-4C. This is a McDonnell F-4B Phantom II (BuNo 153018) of VF-114, CVW-11, USS *Kitty Hawk* (CVA-63), over North Vietnam, March 1968, crewed by pilot Lieutenant Commander Wayne Miller and radar intercept officer (RIO) Lieutenant George Stock. (NHHC)

The US Air Force, US Navy, and US Marine Corps had a commendable range of air-to-air and air-to-ground ordnance, thanks to imaginative naval weapons initiatives over the preceding two decades. These included a family of joint-service bombs and jettisonable tanks – the 250lb Mark 81, 500lb Mark 82, 1,000lb Mark 83, and 2,000lb Mark 84, and 150-, 300-, and 450-gal tanks – all employing the Navy–Douglas Aero 1-A low-drag "scalable" shape. (The Korean War-vintage 750lb Mark 117 and 3,000lb Mark 118 were also extensively employed, particularly by the Air Force.) While these bombs were all generally satisfactory, the Department of Defense possessed too few for its Vietnam needs: by March 1966 the US Air Force in Southeast Asia was dropping 99,900 bombs of all types per month on North and South Vietnam, and Laos, not counting those dropped by the Navy–Marine Corps and RVN Air Force (RVNAF). (At one point, the US Air Force transferred 200 bombs

Republic F-105D Thunderchief (SN 60-464), 44th TFS, 355th TFW carrying six M-117 750lb GP bombs and two Mk 82 500lb bombs. The exceptionally sleek and massive "Thud" bore the brunt of the Air Force's war over the North, but at a fearsome cost in lost aircraft and airmen. (USAF)

A Vought F8U-1 (later F-8A) Crusader (BuNo 143810) of VF-62 catapults off the USS *Enterprise* (CVAN-65) during a demonstration for President John F. Kennedy on April 14, 1962. (NHHC)

per month to the Navy to make up for its bomb shortfalls.) A bomb shortage across the services that year forced the Johnson administration into an embarrassing (and expensive) buy-back of 18,000 bombs sold to other nations for their use or for scrap.

Naval ordnance research after World War II produced a range of air-to-air, air-to-surface, and surface-to-air weapons employed in Vietnam, including the radar-guided Raytheon AIM-7 Sparrow and infrared-guided Raytheon Philco-Ford Aerospace AIM-9 Sidewinder; the Martin AGM-62 Walleye television-guided glide bomb; the rocket-boosted command-guided Martin AGM-12 Bullpup; and the unguided 2.75in Mighty Mouse and 5in Zuni Folding Fin Aerial Rockets (FFAR). Naval vessels boasted three different surface-to-air missiles, the rocket-propelled Convair RIM-2 Terrier and General Dynamics RIM-24 Tartar, and the rocket-boosted ramjet-sustained Bendix RIM-8 Talos.

The chain of command

Rolling Thunder suffered from two great deficiencies: a gradualist and unfocused strategy, combined with convoluted, disjointed, and cumbersome command, control, and execution. The war's rapid expansion after 1964 imposed numerous organizational and procedural changes, such as Pacific Air Forces (PACAF) redesignating the 2nd Air Division as the Seventh Air Force (Seventh AF) in 1966. The chain of command grew increasingly complex, exacerbated by contentious (and always delicate) relations with South Vietnam, Laos, Cambodia, and Thailand.

Far worse was the Johnson–McNamara team's intrusion in operational and even tactical planning and execution, with little if any regard for the existing military chain of command. For example, in July 1964, President Johnson placed General Maxwell Taylor (immediate past Chairman of the Joint Chiefs of Staff and newly appointed American Ambassador to South Vietnam, succeeding Henry Cabot Lodge) in charge of all matters, civil and military, relating to South Vietnam. In this extraordinary authorization, which went well outside the established military chain of command from Washington via Hawaii to Saigon, Johnson granted Taylor broader powers and responsibilities than those possessed and enjoyed by the then-Commander-in-Chief Pacific (CINCPAC), Admiral Ulysses S. Grant Sharp.

"As you take charge of the American effort in South Vietnam, I want you to have this formal expression not only of my confidence, *but of my desire that you have and exercise full responsibility*

The Douglas A-4 (formerly A4D) Skyhawk was a small and versatile single-engine attack bomber that bore the brunt of the naval air war. Flak-vulnerable, the A-4 suffered the Navy's highest combat losses, but it was still much loved by its pilots. This Douglas A-4E Skyhawk (BuNo 151130) is photographed at the Naval Air Test Center, Patuxent River, Maryland, August 29, 1967, carrying a typical SEA bombload. (NHHC)

for the effort of the U.S. Government in South Vietnam," Johnson wrote, adding "I wish it clearly understood that this overall responsibility *includes the whole military effort in South Vietnam and authorizes the degree of command and control that you consider appropriate* … This letter *rescinds all conflicting instructions to U.S. Officers* in Vietnam." [Emphasis added.]

Sharp subsequently enjoyed harmonious relations with Taylor, though in a Vietnam memoir – tellingly entitled *Strategy for Defeat* – he warned that such "broad authority" worked only because of both men's similar backgrounds as career military professionals. If granted to an individual lacking such a background, Sharp warned, ignoring chain of command risked "being extremely disadvantageous to the efficient prosecution of military operations."

At *Rolling Thunder*'s peak, "chain of command" ran from President Lyndon Johnson to Secretary of Defense Robert McNamara; down to General Earle Wheeler, USA, Chairman of the Joint Chiefs of Staff (CJCS); down from the JCS to Pacific Command (PACOM) and its commander (CINCPAC, initially Admiral Ulysses Grant Sharp and then Admiral John McCain, Jr); and thence to the commanders of Pacific Air Forces (CINCPACAF,

The two-place twin-engine Grumman A-6A/B Intruder was the finest all-weather attack aircraft of its time, with a bombing and navigation avionics system enabling pin-point attack. It served in a variety of roles including all-weather night-and-day deep strike, SAM suppression, and battlefield air support. It was rugged and surprisingly agile, though its avionics challenged maintainers. This A-6A (BuNo 152635) of VMA (AW) 533 returns with empty racks to Chu Lai, South Vietnam, on December 15, 1967. (USMC)

McDonnell F-4B Phantom II (BuNo 151408) of VF-143, CVW-14, USS *Constellation* (CVA-64) firing 5in Zunis, a much more precise FFAR. The longer-ranging and more stable Zuni was a worthy successor to the famous 5in High-Velocity Aerial Rocket (HVAR) that had seen extensive service in the latter stages of World War II, in Korea, and in Indochina. (NHHC)

The rocket-boosted ramjet-powered Bendix RIM-8 Talos shipboard SAM could fly over 100 miles at speeds faster than Mach 2.5. Talos shot down two MiGs during *Rolling Thunder*. (NHHC)

initially General Hunter Harris, Jr, followed by General John Ryan, and then General Joseph Nazzaro), Pacific Fleet (CINCPACFLT, initially Admiral Thomas H. Moorer, then Admiral Roy Johnson, followed by Admiral John Hyland), and Military Assistance Command Vietnam (COMUSMACV, initially General William Westmoreland, USA, then General Creighton Abrams, USA).

Contradictions abounded. For example, PACAF's administrative and operational control over Seventh Air Force in Vietnam and Thirteenth Air Force in the Philippines was more complex than organization charts suggested, for it was split and shared in theater based on geographic location. The Seventh AF had administrative control over Vietnamese-based units, while Thirteenth AF had administrative control over those in Thailand. When Seventh AF and Thirteenth AF operated over North Vietnam, their aircraft came under PACOM via PACAF, but if they operated over South Vietnam (which the Seventh AF did routinely, and the Thirteenth AF far less), they came under MACV. Duplicate command posts existed in Saigon, one for "in-country" operations and the other for "out-country" ones. Thai government officials insisted that higher operational command for aircraft flown from Thai bases be located in-country, causing the Air Force to create a "dual-hatted" Thai-based Seventh/Thirteenth AF Deputy Commander. Marines flew from Chu Lai and Da Nang in South Vietnam, their squadrons controlled by four specialized Marine

OPPOSITE SEA COMMAND AND CONTROL RELATIONSHIPS DURING ROLLING THUNDER

Air Groups (MAG) of the 1st Marine Air Wing (1st MAW), the air component of the III Marine Amphibious Force (III MAF), under MACV. (One F-8 squadron served with TF-77, aboard *Oriskany*.) In Laos, to the frustration of General Momyer, a succession of American ambassadors ran its in-country air war, approving air strikes, choice of targets, strike priorities, and rules of engagement, and referring Lao air support requests to the Seventh AF, even though Seventh AF ostensibly controlled joint-service Laotian operations. "Thus," air power strategist Colonel Philip Meilinger wrote, "from one day to the next, aircraft and their crews could fly against targets in three different countries, be controlled by two different agencies, and receive targets from two other agencies. No one was in overall charge. It was extremely confusing."

Strategic Air Command (SAC) planning, targeting, or B-52 strike scheduling likewise bypassed Seventh AF, being overseen by MACV's Air Deputy and a SAC Advanced Echelon (ADVON), in coordination with SAC Headquarters at Offutt AFB, and the Joint Chiefs of Staff. Even MACV's Air Deputy had limited power, unlike a Joint Force Air Component Commander (JFACC) in the 1990s. TF-77 coordinated operations with Seventh Air Force, but otherwise operated independently. Each carrier had an Air Wing Commander (still called "CAG," a reference to the days of Carrier Air Groups) who led the Air Wing (CVW), and reported to the ship's captain, who might or might not be himself a naval aviator.

Given all these varied factors, a postwar RAND study concluded that Vietnam command and control "would have led to disaster if US forces had faced a capable air opponent."

Preparing for the wrong war

The size, mass, and technological superiority of American forces masked a decade of doctrinal, training, and acquisition deficiencies. After Korea, the Air Force (and, to a lesser extent, the Navy) emphasized nuclear attack and defense, while the Army (and even the Marines) trained for the nuclear battlefield. By 1961, preparing for nuclear wars had reduced the services' ability to wage conventional ones.

While the Martin B-57 Canberra, Douglas B-66 Destroyer, Boeing B-52 Stratofortress, Douglas A-1 Skyraider, Douglas A-3 Skywarrior, Douglas A-4 Skyhawk, Grumman A-6 Intruder, McDonnell F-4 Phantom II, and Vought F-8 Crusader largely met the challenges of Southeast Asian combat, the US Air Force's 4,918 supersonic "Century Series" fighters and interceptors – the North American F-100 Super Sabre, McDonnell F-101 Voodoo, Convair F-102 Delta Dagger, Lockheed F-104 Starfighter, Republic F-105 Thunderchief, and Convair F-106 Delta Dart – were less suitable, excepting 1,071 aging workhorse F-100Ds, fighter-bombers in the tradition of World War II or Korea. The rest, having been designed primarily for quick-reaction, high-speed low-level nuclear attack and/or nuclear defense, were less maneuverable than their more agile MiG-17 and MiG-21 opponents, and, lacking sufficient armor and defensive aids (at least when *Rolling Thunder* commenced) were compromised when undertaking missions such as conventional strike deep into the heart of dense antiaircraft defenses.

Though Air Force and naval airmen were true military elites, their readiness for waging conventional air wars had declined sharply after Korea, in part because service doctrine minimized the likelihood of such conflicts. By Vietnam, Air Force fighter pilots rarely shot at towed targets or fired air-to-air missiles, and when they did, only under benign, tail-chase, wings-level, 1g firing conditions, targeting non-maneuvering drones, or drifting parachute flares, an artificial environment far removed from the realities of jet-age air combat.

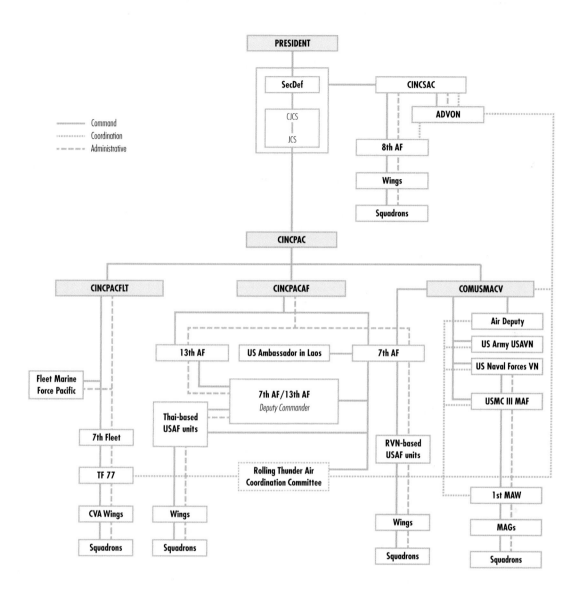

Concerned over safety, commanders minimized aggressive air-to-air hassling. "Between 1954 and 1962, the USAF training curriculum for fighter pilots included little, if any, air-to-air combat," General Bruce K. Holloway (a World War II fighter ace) admitted in 1968, adding "This omission was partly a result of doctrine, which then regarded tactical fighters primarily as a means for delivering nuclear ordnance."

But things changed little even after the Air Force was battling in Vietnamese skies. "It would be a gross understatement to say that F-4 crews left the RTU [F-4 Replacement Training Unit] unprepared for the air-to-air combat some would experience over North Vietnam," Colonel Dick Anderegg wrote long afterwards; "Throughout the war years, air-to-air training was on-again, off-again. Mostly it was off."

As well, after Korea, the military services generally neglected tactical electronic warfare, and so American strike aircraft lacked radar warning receivers, jamming pods, or anti-radar missiles. "SAC had extensive ECM [electronic countermeasure] equipment, but even though SAMs had been in the Soviet air defense system for a number of years, we fighter people were slow to accept the fact that it would take more than maneuverability and speed to defeat a SAM defense system," Seventh AF commander General William "Spike" Momyer recalled. High initial losses forced development of new weapons, equipment, tactics, and the formation of dedicated anti-SAM combat programs such as Iron Hand and Wild Weasel.

In sum, for all its apparent strengths, when America went to war in Vietnam, its military forces were ill prepared to wage an extended Asian war mixing low-intensity conflict; garrison and hamlet protection; mass force-on-force encounters across terrain far different than that of Western Europe; maritime blockade, interdiction, and riverine operations; sustained air support and supply; high-tempo air warfare in an intensive, dynamic, and high-threat environment; all while being politically constrained far greater even than Korea over a decade previously.

US AIR ORDER OF BATTLE, JULY–AUGUST 1965			
USAF PACIFIC AIR FORCES (PACAF) | HICKAM AFB, HI, GEN HUNTER HARRIS USAF, COMMANDING			
Thirteenth Air Force: Clark AB, Philippines | MajGen Sam Maddux USAF, commanding			
2nd Air Division: Tan Son Nhut AB, RVN | MajGen Joseph H. Moore, Jr USAF, commanding			
Location	Subordinate Units	Aircraft	No.
Bien Hoa RVN	6251st Tactical Fighter Wing	F-100D/F	54
		A-1E	48
	38th Air Rescue Squadron Det 6	HH-43B/F	4
Da Nang RVN	405th Air Division	B-57B	24
	476th Tactical Fighter Squadron	F-104C/D	14
	38th Air Rescue Squadron Det 7	HU-16B	2
Tan Son Nhut RVN	481st Tactical Fighter Squadron	F-100D/F	18
	552nd AEWCW Det Project Big Eye	EC-121D	5
	33rd Tactical Group Det 1:		
	Project Able Mable	RF-101C	12
	41st Tac Recon Sqdn Det 1	RB-66B	4
	Project Patricia Lynn	RB-57E	3
Office of the Deputy Commander, 2nd Air Division | Udorn RTAB, Thailand BrigGen John H. McCreery USAF, commanding			
Korat RTAFB	6234th Tactical Fighter Wing	F-105D/F	54
	38th Air Rescue Squadron Det 4	HC-54D	3
Nakhon Phanom RTAFB	38th Air Rescue Squadron Det 1	CH-53C	2
Takhli RTAFB	6235th Tactical Fighter Wing	F-105D/F	36
	9th Tactical Recon Squadron Det 1	RB-66C	9
	38th Air Rescue Squadron Det 2	HH-43B/F	4
Ubon RTAFB	45th Tactical Fighter Squadron	F-4C	18
	38th Air Rescue Squadron Det 3	HH-43B/F	4
Udorn RTAFB	35th Tactical Group Det 2: Project Green Python	RF-101C	12
	33rd Air Rescue Squadron Det	HH-43B/F	4
	36th/79th Air Rescue Squadron Det 5	HC-54D	3
Other USAF units supporting Rolling Thunder			
Location	Unit	Aircraft	No
Bien Hoa RVN	4025th Strategic Recon Sqdn	DC-130A (Drone Recon)	2
Bien Hoa RVN	4028th Strategic Recon Sqdn	U-2D (Reconnaissance)	3
Kadena AFB, Okinawa	4252nd Strategic Wing	KC-135A (Refueling)	45
Don Muang RTAFB	4252nd SW Det Tiger Cub	KC-135A (Refueling)	4

US NAVY PACIFIC FLEET (PACFLT)	PEARL HARBOR, HI	ADM ROY L. JOHNSON USN, COMMANDING		
Seventh Fleet	Yokosuka, Japan	Vice Adm Paul P. Blackburn USN, commanding		
Carrier Task Force 77	In port, Cubi Point, Philippines; at sea, on Yankee Station, or at Dixie Station	Rear Adm Edward C. Outlaw USN, commanding		
Carrier	CVW	Aircraft
Bon Homme Richard (CVA-31)	CVW-19	A-4C (30); A-1H/J (13); F-8E (22); RF-8A (3); E-1B (3, AEW/C2); EA-1F (3, ECM/ECCM); EA-3B (3, SIGINT); UH-2A/B (3, Plane Guard/CSAR)
Oriskany (CVA-34)	CVW-16	A-4E (29); A-1H/J (12); F-8E (25); RF-8A (3) E-1B (3, AEW/C2); EA-1F (3, ECM/ECCM); EA-3B (3, SIGINT); Type Uncertain, likely USMC RF-8A (3, Reconnaissance); UH-2A / UH-2B (3, Plane Guard/CSAR)
Midway (CVA-41)	CVW-2	A-4C/E (28); A-1H/J (12); A-3B (9); F-4B (11); F-8D (12); RA-3B (3); RF-8A (2); E-1B (4, AEW/C2); EA-1F (3, ECM/ECCM); EA-3B (3, SIGINT); UH-2A (3, Plane Guard/CSAR)
Coral Sea (CVA-43)	CVW-15	A 4C/E (27); A 1H/J (12); A-3B (9); F-4B (12); F-8D (14); RA-3B (3); RF-8A (2); E-1B (3, AEW/C2); EA-1F (3, ECM/ECCM); EA-3B (3, SIGINT); UH-2A/UH-2B (4, Plane Guard/CSAR)
Independence (CVA-62)	CVW-7	A-4E (27); A-6A (11); A-3B (3); F-4B (23); RA-3B (3); RA-5C (4); E-1B (4, AEW/C2); EA-1F (3, ECM/ECCM); EA-3B (3, SIGINT); UH-2A (3, Plane Guard/CSAR)
Other USN squadrons with land-planes supporting Rolling Thunder				

Location	Squadrons	Purposes	Aircraft Types	No
NAS Agana, Guam	VW-1	Weather Recon/AEW	EC-121K	7
NAF Atsugi, Japan	VQ-1	SIGINT	EC-121M	4

US MILITARY ASSISTANCE COMMAND, VIETNAM (MACV)	SAIGON, RVN	GEN WILLIAM C. WESTMORELAND, COMMANDING				
III Marine Amphibious Force (III MAF)	Da Nang, RVN	MAJGEN Lewis W. Walt USMC, commanding				
First Marine Aircraft Wing, Advance Echelon, 1st MAW (ADV)	Da Nang, RVN	BrigGen Keith B. McCutcheon USMC, commanding				
Base	Group	Purposes	Aircraft Types	No
Da Nang, RVN	MAG-11	Fighter-Attack	F-4B	30
		Recon/ECM/ECCM	RF-8A and EF-10B	12
Chu Lai, RVN	MAG-12	Attack	A-4C / A-4E	38 / 20

Notes

Unless a campaign is relatively short, the initial order of battle naturally changes over time, reflecting the pace, intensity, and consequences of combat operations. Rolling Thunder evolved from a pattern of retaliatory strikes, so the characteristic well-considered build-up of military forces associated with the planning of a major campaign was absent. (This constituted one of the first of many mistakes that would come to characterize Rolling Thunder.) Nevertheless, at the onset of Rolling Thunder, the essential elements of the larger campaign, its force-structure, and the relative numbers (and types) of aircraft (both land-based and sea-based) were present.

This "slice in time" of July–August 1965 includes all aircraft types routinely operated initially over the DRV. USMC aircraft are often neglected when considering air operations "Up North," but they played an important role, particularly in furnishing electronic countermeasures (ECM) support and radar jamming for 2nd Air Division and TF-77 strike packages operating into high-threat areas. The USAF Strategic Air Command's B-52 force, deployed to Andersen AFB, Guam, and flying Arc Light strikes over South Vietnam from mid-June 1965 and over Laos from mid-December 1965, is not included as it was not yet striking targets in the North.

DEFENDERS' CAPABILITIES

ADF-VPAF in the mid-1960s

The MiG-17F Fresco-C, a remarkably agile and dangerous fighter; this example, in VPAF markings, is at the National Museum of the USAF. Though not as fast, well-armed or powerful as American fighters, the MiG-17 well suited the VPAF's needs. Light, small, and armed with two 23mm and one 37mm cannon and (rarely) rocket pods, it could out-turn any American jet attack and fighter/interceptor aircraft until the advent of the F-15 and F-16 in the 1970s. (NMUSAF)

In the early fall of 1964, the Democratic Republic of Vietnam (DRV) hardly seemed able to confront the United States in the air. The combined Air Defense Forces-Vietnamese People's Air Force (ADF-VPAF), less than two years old, had approximately 1,425 light, medium, and heavy antiaircraft guns – 12.7mm and 14.5mm heavy machine guns; rapid-fire 37mm and 57mm light cannon, and small numbers of 85mm heavy flak guns – distributed among 14 antiaircraft regiments and a further 14 independent battalions. There were just under 300 prepared AAA firing sites, only approximately 160 of which were active. As yet, the ADF-VPAF lacked any surface-to-air missiles, and though it had three radar regiments, it had only approximately 22 early warning radars and four fire-control ones. It thus lacked a well-integrated air defense network, with trained, experienced personnel operating sufficient numbers of up-to-date early warning, height-finding, and fire-control radars. It possessed only three flying units: the 910th Training Regiment with Yak-18 piston-engine trainers (NATO reporting name Max); the 919th Air Transport Regiment, operating a mix of designs, the most advanced being twin-engine Ilyushin Il-14s (NATO Crate); and the 921st *Sao Do* ("Red Star") Fighter Regiment, flying Soviet MiG-17 and Shenyang J-5 (Chinese-built copies of the MiG-17) fighters (both known in the West as the "Fresco") and MiG-15UTI (Shenyang JJ-2) two-place trainers (NATO Midget).

Early days

Yet, despite their force's small size, inadequate structure, and equipment deficiencies, the ADF-VPAF already had a legacy of tenacity under air assault. In January 1951, Vo Nguyen Giap prematurely launched an offensive to seize Hanoi. At Vinh Yen, French fighters and bombers caught the Viet Minh's 308th Infantry Division in the open, killing hundreds. Giap and his commanders thereafter returned to guerrilla warfare, biding their time building strength and antiaircraft defenses, beginning with their first air defense

At Dien Bien Phu, Viet Minh light flak prevented aircraft such as this ex-USAF Armée de l'Air Douglas B-26C Invader (SN 44-35787) from supporting the garrison. (USAF)

unit, the 612th Company, established in May 1951 with four Soviet 37mm M1939 light cannon furnished by Mao Zedong.

From this small beginning, the Viet Minh's antiaircraft strength, nurtured by the PRC, steadily grew, enabling Giap to establish an antiaircraft regiment, the 367th, in April 1953, commanded by Le Van Tri and assigned to the 351st Heavy Division. The 367th underwent months of extensive training in China before returning to northwest Vietnam in time for the pivotal siege of Dien Bien Phu in the spring of 1954. There, two of its battalions thwarted French attempts to supply the encircled garrison. Flak from approximately 80 M1939 37mm light cannon and an estimated 100 DShK 1938 12.7mm heavy machine guns downed 48 French Armée de l'Air and Aéronavale aircraft and damaged another 167. Massive disparities in opposing artillery and troop strength made the fall of this ill-conceived *"Base Aéro-Terrestre"* ("Air-Land Base") a virtual certainty; but Viet Minh flak sealed Dien Bien Phu's fate.

In March 1949, at the instigation of then-President Ho Chi Minh, Giap had formed a committee to begin shaping a Vietnamese air arm. After the Geneva Accords of 1954, the newly independent DRV inherited former French airfields such as Bac Mai at Hanoi and Cat Bi at Haiphong. Recognizing these as insufficient, planners envisioned up to 42 across the North. In January 1956, the DRV received its first aircraft, Czech Aero Ae-45S light twin-engine trainers and utility aircraft, from the PRC. On March 21, 1958, the DRV's Ministry of National Defense established a specialized Air Defense Command. Over the next several years, the Ministry of Defense sent more than a hundred pilot candidates to training in the PRC and Soviet Union, together with hundreds of other officers and soldiers sent to bases across the USSR for specialist antiaircraft training. It established two flying training schools in Vietnam, formed an Air Force administrative department, created its first operational unit, the 919th Air Transport Regiment (equipped with a mix of single- and-twin-engine Antonov An-2 biplanes, Lusinov Li-2s – a license-built copy of the DC-3 – and the more modern Ilyushin Il-14), and followed this with the formation of the 910th Training Regiment and a central aviation technical training school at Cat Bi. The PAVN sent student pilots to both China and the USSR. Washout-rates were high: on average, only one in five satisfactorily qualified as jet fighter pilots.

By the summer of 1963, the PAVN had eight antiaircraft regiments possessing a mix of 14.5mm, 37mm, 57mm, 85mm, and 100mm cannon. Structured along Soviet lines, each 57mm, 85mm, and 100mm AA regiment typically had four firing batteries of six

An Ilyushin Il-14 (NATO reporting name Crate) photographed on a covert resupply mission to the Pathet Lao. (USAF)

cannon each. Manned by approximately five officers and 60 men, and possessing at least a dozen trucks and eight heavy movers, each battery had its own Whiff and/or Fire Can fire-control radar, PUAZO-6 fire-control director, and a power generator. The ADF-VPAF's radar-cued 57mm, 85mm, and 100mm AAA posed a deadly threat. Firing proximity-fuzed shells, a six-gun 100mm KS-19 battery could fire 86 rounds in the space of 20 seconds, with a kill probability of 60 percent against an airplane at 30,000ft. Low-flying fast aircraft seemingly avoided such risk, but their flight paths took them into the arena of intense light flak and barrage fire: a single 57mm cannon firing for six seconds had a 45 percent kill probability against an airplane flying at 500kt (Mach 0.76) at 1,000ft. The PAVN in 1963 had three radar regiments, though as yet the DRV lacked any sort of comprehensive overarching command-and-control air defense network. A US Navy report that September listed numerous gaps in coverage, in contrast to the Soviet Union, China, and North Korea. But within two years, all this changed: the PAVN rapidly increased the numbers and quality of its radars, blessed by generous Soviet assistance. As with its elite 228B flak regiment, the PAVN employed the 291st Radar Regiment to groom operators and technicians.

North Vietnam's Air Defense Forces

On October 22, 1963, the Ministry of Defense amalgamated its antiaircraft and aviation forces under a single headquarters, the Air Defense Forces of Vietnam-Vietnamese People's Air Force (ADF-VPAF), commanded by Colonel Phung The Tai (born Phung Van Thu), with Colonel Dang Tinh as deputy commander. By then, the ADF-VPAF possessed 83 aircraft: 44 transports, a dozen helicopters, and 27 trainers. On February 3, 1964, the Soviet Union gifted the DRV with 36 MiG-17s and MiG-15 UTI trainers. That same day, Lieutenant General Hoang Van Thai, Deputy Minister of Defense, established the 921st Fighter Regiment, under the command of Lieutenant Colonel Dao Dinh Luyen. Then

based at Mong Tu, China, it consisted of two companies of MiG-17 Fresco-As supported by one technical company.

Overall, the VPAF received approximately 270 MiG-17s and Shenyang J-5s, roughly 240 of which were afterburner-equipped Fresco-Cs. MiG-17 strength peaked over 1966–67 when – sources vary – the VPAF fielded anywhere from 45 to 75 at any one time. Knife Rest, Bar Lock, and Flat Face early warning and ground control radars paired to Side Net height-finders cued VPAF ground controllers to vector flights of three or four MiGs to engage American aircraft.

Air Force and Navy airmen found the Fresco-C a challenge because its small size and clean exhaust made it difficult to see, while its afterburner-sustained turns in a close-in "fur-ball" could be lethal. "That little airplane can give you a tussle the likes of which you've never had before in your life," Colonel Robin Olds, *Rolling Thunder*'s most successful fighter pilot, told a study team in 1967, adding "Their turn radius has to be seen to be believed. It's incredible."

Offsetting its strengths was a poor gunsight, slow-firing cannon whose low muzzle velocity (2,250ft/sec), forced large target-leading compensation, and a limited flying time of about 25 minutes in clean configuration. Though unmatched in turning, the MiG-17 ran out of energy if forced into the vertical. At least at first, the VPAF's MiG pilots generally had poor gunnery skills, poor flight discipline (wingmen and leaders routinely abandoned each other, and frequently ran out of fuel), and an over-dependence upon jam-vulnerable ground-controlled intercept (GCI) tactics. All this reflected badly on their Soviet training, which the CIA judged "unimaginative and stultifying … rigid and unrealistic [with] pilots still closely wedded to ground control at all times."

Two dispersed MiG-17Fs at Phuc Yen in 1966, together with (at upper far left) a MiG-15UTI Midget two-place trainer. (USAF)

The VPAF operated both the Soviet Fresco-C and its Chinese equivalent, the Shenyang J-5. Here is a PLAAF J-5, whose pilot defected to Taiwan. (Author)

From the fall of 1963 onwards, responding to DRV, Viet Cong, and Pathet Lao provocations, the Johnson administration fitfully expanded America's regional military presence. Worried, the PAVN Chief of Staff, General Van Tien Dung, visited Beijing in June 1964. Mao Zedong promised to send Chinese troops into the DRV if the United States ever invaded, adding "Your business is my business and my business is your business." In July, PRC premier Zhou Enlai visited Hanoi, reaffirming Mao's promise of the previous month to furnish small arms, artillery, antiaircraft cannon, other supplies and material, and even "volunteers" if needed.

Then, on August 2, 1964, came the Tonkin Gulf incident: three DRV P-4 torpedo boats unsuccessfully attacked the destroyer USS *Maddox* (DD-731), steaming off-shore on an intelligence-gathering patrol. After a second non-existent "attack" – reflecting jittery nerves and misread sensor data – seemingly took place two days later, President Lyndon Johnson ordered retaliatory air strikes, Operation *Pierce Arrow*. On August 7, the Congress passed a resolution authorizing Johnson to employ whatever military force the administration thought necessary, effectively launching America's full and open participation in what was now the Vietnam War.

The Tonkin Gulf attack and American response triggered ADF-VPAF adjustment. On August 6, 16 Frescos of the 921st Fighter Regiment relocated from Mong Tu to Noi Bai (Phuc Yen). There, regiment commander Luyen initiated an aggressive training program: 921st pilots flew more over the next four months at Phuc Yen than over the previous year at Mong Tu. As well, Ho Chi Minh visited the unit on November 11, 1964, exhorting its pilots to "open up a victorious battlefront in the air."

Anticipating strikes on Hanoi and Haiphong, Colonel Phung The Tai redeployed the ADF-VPAF's AA forces. He recalled the 234th regiment from Laos; formed a new reserve regiment, the 212th; pulled three AA battalions from three divisions and deployed them across the Vinh military region; and moved two AA regiments, the 213th and 214th, to defend Ninh Bình province and Vinh itself. In November, the ADF-VPAF formed the first of many ambush "clusters," locating the 213th, 228th, and 230th AA Regiments around Mai Su, under a single commander: Dien Bien Phu veteran Le Van Tri.

After Tonkin Gulf, China and the Soviet Union accelerated their aid. Mao already had sent 18 aircraft; 80,500 guns and 25 million bullets; 1,200 artillery pieces and 335,000 rounds; and much other equipment: now China delivered a further 72 aircraft; 730,000 guns and 687 million bullets, 18,900 artillery pieces and 6.3 million rounds; and other supplies. (As well, between June 1965 and March 1968, 320,000 PLA specialists and troops served in the DRV on antiaircraft, road-railroad-and-bridge repair, and factory construction.)

Strengths and weaknesses

By the end of *Rolling Thunder*, however, the DRV had turned decisively towards the USSR. The bitter China–Soviet rivalry had hindered aid deliveries. China did not permit "through" Soviet airlift, and, after the onset of the "Cultural Revolution," rival factions often held up or even seized Soviet aid sent by rail. (On two occasions, the CIA reported "trainloads" of SAMs delayed at the Sino-Soviet border.) Though Soviet premier Nikita Khrushchev – leery of antagonizing the United States – had offered the DRV little but verbal support, his successors Alexei Kosygin and Leonid Brezhnev readily assented to Hanoi's requests.

On November 17, 1964 the Politburo approved sending advisors and SAMs to the DRV, the first 70 arriving by ship in April 1965. Over *Rolling Thunder*, Soviet military aid totaled $1.05 billion (equivalent in 2017 to $8.1 billion), typified by MiGs, missiles, and radars. First delivered to the DRV in 1965, the Soviet Vympel S-75 Dvina (NATO SA-2 Guideline)

A Soviet Vympel S-75 Dvina (NATO SA-2 Guideline) surface-to-air missile. The rail-launched S-75 had a solid-fuel first-stage booster and a second-stage sustainer burning a hypergolic (self-igniting) fuel and oxidizer mix. Over 35ft long, this radio-guided missile had a peak velocity over Mach 3 (≈1,722kts), an effective range of approximately 18 miles, and an effective height up to 85,000ft. It had a 420lb proximity-fuzed warhead with impact fuze and command detonation backup. The lethal blast diameter varied from 200ft in the denser lower atmosphere to 800ft at 35,000ft. (NARA)

BELOW LAYOUT OF A TYPICAL SA-2 SITE

Six launchers (**1**) were placed around a central Fan Song radar (**2**) and its control van (**3**). Each launcher pointed outwards and was protected by an earth berm (**4**) bulldozed into place around it. Support vehicles for logistics and communications (**5**) were clustered around the Fan Song. Bamboo matting was often used to cover the mud roads (**6**) around the site, to allow missile transporters (**7**) easier access to the launchers.

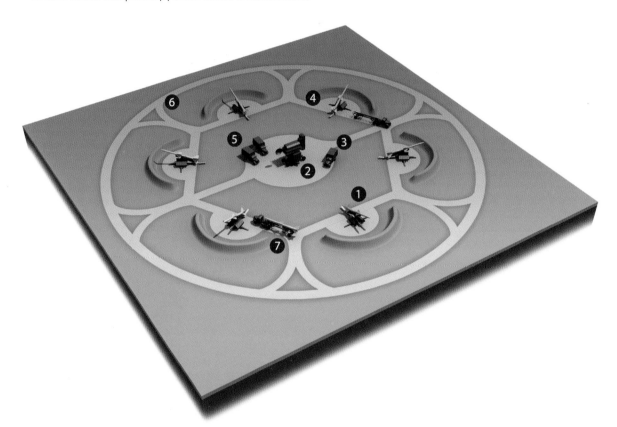

surface-to-air missile and the MiG-21 (NATO Fishbed) family constituted the most significant Soviet additions to its air defense force. Soviet PVO-Strany (the Soviet Union's air defense force) personnel from the Moscow and Baku military districts, commanded by General Major Grigoriy Belov, trained and supported the ADF-VPAF's missileers; through 1973, 17,114 Soviet military and civil personnel served in Vietnam, mostly in air defense.

Emulating Soviet practice, a DRV SA-2 regiment had three battalions, each firing battery comprised of six individual mobile launchers arranged in a revealing six-pointed-star formation, with a Spoon Rest search radar and a Fan Song fire-control radar at the center, and with command, communication, and supporting vans, vehicles, missile transporters, and a crane around the periphery. The regiment's headquarters target acquisition/early warning section typically maintained a Flat Face search radar and a Side Net height-finder. After receiving warning of an approaching aircraft from a Bar Lock or Knife Rest, the Spoon Rest acquired the target, passed its range, bearing, and altitude – the latter furnished by the Side Net – to the Fan Song, which tracked the target – indeed, up to six simultaneously – and, if the battery commander launched missiles against it, guided as many as three S-75s to intercept it. After firing, a five-person team could reload each launcher in approximately 15 minutes. Without fanfare, on 7 October 1959, the SA-2 claimed its first victim (a Nationalist Chinese Martin RB-57D flying near Beijing); but it burst on the world

scene with its second, Gary Powers' Lockheed U-2C shot down over Sverdlovsk on May 1, 1960 with a characteristic three-missile salvo that also fatally claimed a climbing MiG-19 (NATO Farmer) and its unlucky pilot.

The MiG-21F-13, a simple, reliable, tailed-delta interceptor with performance roughly comparable to the American Starfighter, British Lightning, French Mirage, and Swedish Draken, gave the VPAF a genuine supersonic fighter (over Mach 2 in "clean" configuration), one armed with a single 30mm cannon and two Atoll AAMs, and a simple SRD-5ND Kvant (NATO High Fix) gun-laying radar. Overall, its small size and smokeless exhaust made it difficult to detect beyond two miles, and this, combined with high top-end speed and an effective missile armament made the MiG-21F-13 and its later Spin Scan equipped successors dangerous threats.

Yet the Fishbed's initially impressive performance masked serious deficiencies. Its thick armored glass, gunsight, and windscreen framing limited the pilot's forward vision and its ogival body restricted over-the-nose vision, while the ejection seat restricted his rearward perspective. Its light structure forced imposition of a 614kt (Mach 0.98) limit below 15,000ft, while stabilator loads and stick forces at this altitude limited longitudinal (pitch) control response. Its single 30mm cannon had only 60 rounds, and the optical lead-computing gunsight had such jitter – in excess of 20 mils – during firing, and sight reticule drifting during maneuvering, that MiG-21 evaluators in 1969 concluded "target tracking is impossible over 3-gs." Unlike the earlier swept-wing MiG-17, the MiG-21's commendably high instantaneous turn rate came with rapid energy bleed-off – a characteristic of all delta-wing aircraft – leaving it slow and vulnerable, a situation made worse because its engine acceleration was excessively long. It had poor directional stability, something rectified in later models by increasing the area of the vertical fin. Finally, its light structure, lack of self-sealing fuel tanks, absence of armor protection for vital systems (excepting the cockpit, which was well protected) and high-pressure air storage bottles ensured that the Fishbed, unlike the robust MiG-17, was easily destroyed if hit.

In February 1965, after a series of Viet Cong attacks against Bien Hoa air base, a Saigon hotel used as a US officers' quarters, Camp Holloway at Pleiku (destroying or damaging 24 aircraft), and an enlisted billet at Quy Nhon, the United States and Republic of Vietnam launched two waves of retaliatory air strikes, Operations *Flaming Dart I* and *II*, against North Vietnam by Air Force, Navy, and South Vietnamese aircraft.

Following these strikes, Vice Premier Le Thanh Nghi ordered the expansion of airfields at Hoa Lac, Yen Bai, Tho Xuan, Kép, Gia Lam, and Kien An. The ADF-VPAF established GCI stations at Kien An, Tho Xuan, and Vinh airfields; formed three new AA regiments, the 212th, 216th, and 222nd, and a new AA division, 361st, to defend Hanoi; and moved other AA units to cover key bridges and the China–Vietnam railway. Communist Party cadres mobilized hundreds of students, instructors, and professionals in universities and polytechnics to attend a newly formed radar school at Ha Tay, where Soviet instructors trained them on Spoon Rests, Bar Locks, and Side Nets. It formed a bomber squadron, the 929th, equipped with eight Ilyushin Il-28 (NATO Beagle) light twin-jet bombers (roughly equivalent to the British Canberra and its American derivative, the B-57).

Finally, in the spring of 1965, after *Rolling Thunder* had commenced, the DRV established its first S-75 Regiment, the 236th, under Colonel Nguyen Quang Tuyen, locating two of its launch batteries around Hanoi. Other changes would come over time – creation of more SAM regiments and a second MiG-17/J-5 fighter regiment (the 923rd) at Kép, under Major Nguyen Phuc Trach; introduction of the MiG-21F-13 and later more capable models; and changes in administration and organization – but by the spring of 1965 the basic framework and infrastructure of the DRV's air defense network and capabilities was in place: *Rolling Thunder* would not go unopposed, and opposition would be vigorous.

The Soviet Ilyushin Il-28 (NATO Beagle) light twin-engine bomber. Their presence caused concern and they were targeted in several 1968 air raids. (JFKL)

NORTH VIETNAMESE AIR ORDER OF BATTLE, JULY–AUGUST 1965				
Air Defense Forces-Vietnamese People's Air Force | Hanoi, DRV Colonel Phung The Tai, commanding | Political Commissar Senior Colonel Dang Tinh				
VPAF Flying Units[1]				
Base	Unit	Purposes	Aircraft Types	No
Phuc Yen	921st Fighter Regiment	Air Defense	MiG-17/-17F/JJ-5	≈30
	929th Bomber Squadron	Medium Attack	Ilyushin Il-28	8
Kép	923rd Fighter Regiment	Air Defense	MiG-17/-17F/JJ-5	≈30
Gia Lam	919th Transport Regiment[2]	Air Mobility, SOF	Il-14, Li-2, An-2, Mi-4	≈50
Antiaircraft Forces, Large and Small				
Note: At the beginning of 1965, the DRV's AA forces consisted of 3 radar regiments, 14 AA regiments, and 14 independent AA battalions; by year's end, it had added 1 radar regiment, and 3 additional AA regiments. Known AA and SAM regiments as of the late summer of 1965 are listed below. Many more were formed subsequently: by February 1967 the ADF possessed 10 SAM regiments, 23 AA regiments, 15 independent AA battalions, and its 4 radar regiments had a total of 37 radar companies distributed across the North.				
AA Regiments: 210, 212, 213, 214, 216, 222, 224, 226, 228, 228B, 230, 233, 234, 241, 255, 260, 270, 280	For defense of Hanoi, Haiphong, Vinh, & Panhandle; some mixed in "forward" mobile air defense clusters			
Radar Regiments: 290, 291, 292, 293	Operating early warning and fire-control radars			
Ground Observer Corps	Militia and Party cadre-run			
PAVN/Militia air defense forces	Armed with heavy machine guns and light weapons			
236th Missile Regiment[3]	First S-75 (SA-2) regiment, Colonel M. Tsygankov, commanding			
238th Missile Regiment	Second S-75 (SA-2) regiment, Colonel N. V. Bazhenov, commanding			

1 Not including the 910th Training Regiment which was based at Gia Lam but could not play a role in the direct air defense of the DRV; neither are the MiG-15UTI trainers counted as well.

2 The 919th's transports maintained a constant resupply of weapons and ammunition to deployed ADF-VPAF antiaircraft forces and therefore are counted as air defense assets; in 1968, four 919th An-2s attacked Lima Site 85, a forward-based USAF radar bombing control site, with two shot down by an Air America UH-1 helicopter.

3 SA-2 regiments only as of July–August 1965; again, as with conventional AA regiments, many more added subsequently.

CAMPAIGN OBJECTIVES
Trying not to win

President John F. Kennedy meeting with Secretary of Defense Robert S. McNamara (right) and Secretary of State Dean Rusk (left), January 23, 1961. (JFKL)

For America and North Vietnam, the summer and fall of 1964 mixed worries and hopes. Anxious over the Presidential election in early November, Lyndon Johnson reassured Americans "We don't want our American boys to do the fighting for Asian boys" even as he and his national security team contemplated employing graduated air and naval pressure to coerce the Ho regime into ceasing support of the Viet Cong and Pathet Lao.

Ho Chi Minh, Vo Nguyen Giap, and the PAVN's leaders already believed Johnson would bomb airfields, bases, bridges, roads, rail lines, petroleum storage, power plants, industrial plants, ports (particularly Haiphong), and Hanoi. Could they inflict sufficient losses to end the bombing? And could their labor and militia prevent disruption of the Ho Chi Minh Trail, which criss-crossed southern North Vietnam and Laos, below the 19th Parallel?

Gradualism and the "tragic mistake"

During the 1960 campaign, John Kennedy had criticized Dwight Eisenhower for offering only a choice between "world devastation or submission." Once President, he tasked Secretary of Defense Robert McNamara to develop "graduated pressure" via conventional (i.e. non-nuclear) force. In response, in April 1961 the US Air Force launched Project Jungle Jim, counterinsurgency (COIN) training for carefully selected airmen in propeller-driven Douglas B-26s, North American T-28s, and Douglas C-47s. That October, Kennedy ordered a detachment sent to Vietnam. Codenamed Farm Gate, its first 155 airmen, eight T-28s, and four B-26s arrived at Bien Hoa in November. From this small beginning grew a 14-year USAF entanglement in Vietnam.

The Laotian accords signed in 1962 inadvertently accelerated infiltration down the Ho Chi Minh Trail, and the Viet Cong enjoyed alarming new battlefield success. South Vietnam's President Ngo Dình Diem, an ardent nationalist and pious Catholic, had worked to build a strong, independent, and modern country, assisted by his hardline brother Ngo

Two VNAF North American T-28C Trojans (BuNos. 140457 and 140556) over Vietnam, October 1962. Note the underwing .50-cal gun pods. (USAF)

Dinh Nhu and fiery sister-in-law. Diem frustrated French hopes of controlling the new state, defeated corrupt political sects and criminal gangs, confronted the Viet Cong, and confounded political rivals including ambitious Buddhists, scheming generals, and radical students. Still, over 1963 unrest grew, stoked by the Ho regime. In response, Diem and Nhu launched a harsh crackdown that backfired badly – several protesting monks immolated themselves – and discontent soared.

By late summer 1963, Kennedy's team concluded Diem must distance himself from the Nhus or step down, encouraging ambitious generals to plan a coup. They struck on November 1. Diem and Nhu evaded capture, were promised safe passage out of the country by Ambassador Henry Cabot Lodge, surrendered to the ARVN, and then were brutally murdered, apparently on the orders of General Duong Van "Big" Minh. "I can scarcely believe the Americans would be so stupid," Ho Chi Minh reputedly said. "That was a *tragic* mistake," President Lyndon Johnson emphasized in a telephone conversation with Senate leader Richard Russell in May 1964, adding both accurately and presciently "It was awful and we've lost everything." Certainly the murders tarnished America's image in Asia, triggering further travails and cabals.

In March 1964, Admiral Harry Felt, commander of US Pacific forces (CINCPAC) had a plan prepared targeting the DRV's known military capabilities; Secretary of State Dean Rusk believed it "emphasized the bombing of the North more than I was entirely comfortable with." Whether to bomb split the JCS: USAF General Curtis LeMay and USMC General Wallace Greene favored a comprehensive campaign, but Army General Harold Johnson, Admiral David McDonald, and Chairman General Maxwell Taylor (CJCS) demurred.

Instead, the JCS offered McNamara three options in mid-April: first, intensified air strikes and ground action in South Vietnam with "hot pursuit" into Laos and Cambodia; second, reprisals into North Vietnam, including air strikes, airborne and amphibious raids, and port and harbor mining; and third, a graduated,

USAF Chief of Staff General Curtis LeMay scorned the Johnson–McNamara–Bundy–Rusk team's gradualism. He retired before the onset of *Rolling Thunder*. (USAF)

One of the attacking MTBs during the August 2, 1964 action. (NHHC)

A Chinese-built Type 55A *Shantou* (NATO Swatow-class) DRV patrol boat burning near Hon Me Island, after attacks on August 5, 1964 by *Constellation's* Carrier Air Wing 14 (CVW-14) during Operation *Pierce Arrow*. (NHHC)

coercive air campaign. *Rolling Thunder* was largely based on the third.

As late as summer 1964, Taylor and General William Westmoreland (newly appointed MACV commander) feared that bombing could trigger Chinese intervention, always a Kennedy–Johnson era policy concern. Lulled by the confident bellicosity of General Nguyen Khanh – who helped unseat Diem, then rallied others to topple "Big" Minh, becoming South Vietnam's third President – both even thought South Vietnam was recovering from its travails.

Tonkin Gulf and its aftermath

On August 2, 1964, three torpedo boats attacked the *Maddox* (DD-731) as it gathered intelligence along the North Vietnamese coast. *Maddox* avoided their torpedoes, and its counterfire, assisted by strafing F-8Es from VF-51 and VF-53 off *Ticonderoga*, sank one boat and sent the others limping into port. Two nights later, *Maddox* – joined by *C. Turner Joy* (DD-951) – again reported an "attack," this time the product of twitchy nerves, faulty intelligence, and misreading sensors. Believing it real, Admiral U. S. Grant Sharp (Felt's successor at PACOM), immediately called for air strikes.

Army General Earle Wheeler, the new Joint Chiefs chairman, supported attacks, as did the Chiefs. Rusk, McNamara, and National Security Advisor McGeorge Bundy urged restraint. Johnson then authorized a limited strike, Operation *Pierce Arrow*. McNamara recommended announcing it at 2200hrs Washington time, giving PAVN flak crews two hours' warning. When Johnson asked with some incredulity "Do we want to give them two hours' notice?" McNamara astonishingly answered "I don't believe there's any reason not to." "I'd sure as hell hate to have some mother say 'You announced it and my boy got killed,'" Johnson replied doubtfully. But McNamara nonchalantly reassured him "I don't think there is much danger of that."

So, on August 5, *Ticonderoga's* and *Constellation's* air wings targeted Quang Khe, Phuc Loi, Loc Chao, and Hong Gai, and a petroleum complex at Vinh. They wrecked or damaged nearly 30 boats, destroying over 90 percent of the Vinh complex, and losing an A-1H and A-4C to flak. LBJ delayed the announcement but, as Lady Bird Johnson confided to her diary, "The exact location of the planes [when he made it] was clouded in confusion." And despite McNamara's glib assurances, an airman did die: VA-145's Lieutenant (jg) Richard C.

Sather, the first American lost over North Vietnam. The A-4 pilot, VA-144's Lieutenant (jg) Everett Alvarez Jr, became the first POW held in the Hoa Lo prison, the soon-infamous "Hanoi Hilton." On August 7, by margins of 416–0 in the House and 88–2 in the Senate, Congress passed the Tonkin Gulf Resolution, authorizing "all necessary measures to repel any armed attack against the forces of the United States and to prevent further aggression."

In March and April 1964, a State Department study, buttressed by a Joint Chiefs' wargame ("SIGMA"), had concluded that air attacks would not coerce the DRV's leaders into abandoning the Viet Cong and Pathet Lao, and might trigger the dreaded Chinese intervention. (A follow-on wargame, SIGMA II, replicated the earlier results.) Still, in May 1964, a JCS Joint Working Group had assembled a list of 99 potential targets, winnowing them to 94 by late August. These included airfields; headquarters, training facilities, and barracks; ammunition, ordnance, and storage depots; petrochemical processing and storage; communications facilities; ports; iron, steel, fertilizer, and thermal power plants; bridges; railyards and repair facilities; and routes warranting "armed reconnaissance," a euphemism for road and trail interdiction. On August 29, John McNaughton, Assistant Secretary of Defense for International Security Affairs (and McNamara's closest advisor) passed the list to the Defense Secretary.

General Hunter Harris, Pacific Air Forces commander at the onset of *Rolling Thunder*, feared that not using air power for maximum effect would discredit it. (USAF)

Politics, strategy, outrages, and reprisals

By turns courtly and coarse, pleasant and profane, cajoling and threatening, Lyndon Johnson had mastered Congressional maneuverings and domestic politics. Facing Senator Barry Goldwater – an outspoken anti-Communist and major general in the Air Force Reserves – he portrayed himself as reasonable, experienced, and moderate, disingenuously proclaiming "We are not going north." Until the election was sorted out, Johnson resisted using force: when the VPAF's MiG-17s relocated from China on August 6, and Admiral Sharp and General Hunter Harris, commander of Pacific Air Forces, urged bombing Phuc Yen, Johnson demurred. As political scientist Gordon Goldstein concluded, "Politics became the enemy of strategy in 1964."

Johnson's refusal to strike Phuc Yen roiled the JCS. Then William Bundy, Assistant Secretary of State for Far Eastern Affairs (and brother of McGeorge Bundy), recommended

A Martin B-57B Canberra (SN 52-1555), destroyed at Bien Hoa in the mortar attack of November 1, 1964. (NMUSAF)

postponing action against the North until early 1965 (and so it was). To LeMay, the failure to take decisive action "nullified" any good accomplished by *Pierce Arrow*.

Sending jet aircraft to South Vietnam and Thailand increased America's regional punch, but set up an enticing target. On November 1, 1964, the Viet Cong mortared Bien Hoa air base, destroying or damaging 20 of 33 Martin B-57B bombers as well as 12 other aircraft, and killing or wounding 76 servicemen.

Taylor, Westmoreland, and the JCS all favored retaliation, differing only in degree. Taylor advocated attacking Phuc Yen and barracks associated with infiltration "preferably within 24 hours, at latest within 48 hours." At a hastily called Sunday meeting the JCS recommended hitting all the targets on their August list. That morning, Wheeler met with McNamara, warning that if the President continued to delay "most of [the JCS] believed the United States should withdraw from South Vietnam." Johnson still would not be moved, his inaction possibly misleading the DRV's leaders. (Rusk concluded, "It's entirely possible that Hanoi said to themselves 'Lyndon Johnson says "we don't want a larger war," therefore, we, Hanoi, can have a larger war without an increase of risk.'")

With the election over, LBJ finally turned hawk, committing to undefined air action, rationalizing that it would signal resolve, boost South Vietnamese morale, and "impose increased costs and strains" upon the DRV. In October, Undersecretary of State George Ball published an article revealing that the administration was "considering air action against [North Vietnam] as the means to a limited objective – the improvement of our bargaining position with the North Vietnamese." This was openly signaling to the DRV the intent, limits, and end-goal – improving negotiation position, not achieving decisive military effect – of any likely campaign. He informed Maxwell Taylor on December 3 that South Vietnam and America should "execute prompt reprisals for any unusual hostile action," including a "series of air attacks on the DRV progressively mounting in scope and intensity for the purpose of convincing the leaders of DRV that it is to their interest to cease to aid the Viet Cong and to respect the independence and security of South Vietnam."

On December 10, 1964, Prince Souvanna Phouma authorized unpublicized armed "road reconnaissance" along three routes crossing the Laotian panhandle. The US Air Force flew its first on December 14; and the Navy followed on the 17th, beginning *Barrel Roll*, a northern Laotian interdiction program lasting the next eight years. (*Steel Tiger*, over southern Laos, followed in April 1965.) Initial restrictions were severe, and (in the words of Air Force analysts in 1967), "induced a stereotyped form of operation, easily analyzed and countered by the enemy." All missions required JCS approval; there was a two-week wait even for pre-planned targets; and re-flights – even for damage assessment! – necessitated a three-day wait.

The Brinks Hotel after the Viet Cong bombing of December 24, 1964. (NMUSAF)

Direct constraints included a prohibition on overflying the DRV; respecting a 2-mile Laotian buffer zone along the DRV border; a prohibition (subsequently lifted) on using napalm "regardless of target;" armed recce strikes only within 200 yards of roads, and direction of armed recce stipulated by the "frag" (operational) order; no attacking secondary targets while on night operations; no employment (at this time) of Thai-based aircraft; and "reseeding" bombing of choke points no earlier than four days after a strike.

"The situation in Vietnam is deteriorating"

On December 22, McNamara, his deputy Cyrus Vance, and the JCS flew to Johnson's Texas ranch. After a morning of meetings on Vietnam, they lunched with Johnson and the First Lady, assembling by the pool for final discussions before returning to Washington. Two days later, on Christmas Eve, the Viet Cong bombed Saigon's Brinks Hotel, an American officers' quarters, killing two and injuring 107. They then ended what had been a very good year for them by defeating the ARVN and South Vietnamese Marines at Bình Giã, even facing down helicopter and fixed-wing air attacks.

Consequently, as Rusk recalled, "As 1965 opened, the military situation in South Vietnam was dire indeed." In his last month as Chief of Staff and thus "getting short," LeMay groused to his fellow chiefs, "For a long time I've said we should go north. Our present strategies aren't working," adding "I don't understand how we can go on as we have." In June 1964, anticipating an expanded war, he'd already ordered SAC's B-52Fs modified to carry racks of conventional bombs on their wing pylons. Now he ordered its B-52Ds modified to carry up to 60,000lb of bombs, using both wing pylons and internal carriage.

By now, even McGeorge Bundy and McNamara realized Johnson must change course. On January 27 Bundy warned him either to expand the war or to disengage. Still noncommittal, Johnson tasked Rusk to explore exit strategies, and Bundy to visit Vietnam and take "a hard look at the situation on the ground."

On February 7, the Viet Cong attacked Camp Holloway at Pleiku, killing or wounding 116 soldiers and destroying or damaging 25 airplanes and helicopters. The attack, while Alexei Kosygin was visiting Hanoi, surprised Moscow: Anatoly Dobrynin, Ambassador to Washington, later accused the DRV's leaders of "doing their utmost to foster enmity between Washington and Moscow," adding "the Soviet leaders were well aware of the game the Vietnamese were playing and cursed them behind their backs."

"The situation in Vietnam is deteriorating, and without new US action defeat appears inevitable," Bundy reported to Johnson:

> To be an American in Saigon today is to have a gnawing feeling that time is against us… We believe that the best available way of increasing our chance of success in Vietnam is the development and execution of a policy of sustained reprisal against North Vietnam… It implies significant US air losses even if no full air war is joined, and it seems likely that it would eventually require an extensive and costly effort against the whole air defense system of North Vietnam. US casualties would be higher – and more visible to American feelings – than those sustained in the struggle in South Vietnam. Yet measured against the costs of defeat in Vietnam, this program seems cheap. And even if it fails to turn the tide – as it may – the value of the effort seems to us to exceed its cost… *The object would not be to 'win' an air war against Hanoi, but rather to influence the course of the struggle in the South."* [Emphasis added]

Unfortunately, that last sentence – the fatal conceit underpinning *Rolling Thunder*'s misguided gradualism – contained within it the essence of the campaign's subsequent failure.

Meeting with McNamara, Wheeler, Vance, Ball, William Bundy, and Senate Majority Leader Mike Mansfield, Johnson acted at last. He told them "the enemy was killing his personnel and he could not expect them to continue

Admiral U. S. Grant Sharp, a non-aviator, nevertheless instinctively understood the importance of using air power decisively, as part of a coherent, effects-based strategy. As CINCPAC he consistently argued for striking meaningful targets, disagreeing with the Johnson administration's gradualist approach. (NHHC)

their work if he did not authorize them to take steps to defend themselves." He authorized Operation *Flaming Dart*, a PACOM reaction plan prepared in case of another Tonkin Gulf-like attack. *Coral Sea* and *Hancock* struck barracks complexes around Dong Hoi, flak claiming one A-4E and its pilot. Bad weather prevented a *Ranger* strike on Vit Thu Lu. Fearing collisions amidst various flights smothering Dong Hoi, VNAF chief Nguyen Cao Ky diverted his Skyraider flight to Ho Xa, losing two A-1s to flak, and being slightly wounded himself.

On February 9, the Viet Cong bombed an enlisted billet in Quy Nhon, killing 23 and triggering *Flaming Dart II* on February 11. Its execution revealed the growing disjointedness between Washington and Saigon. PACAF analysts subsequently wrote:

> 2d Air Division originally received a target list from a MACV planning conference held on 10 February. Three hours were spent on planning for the strike on this target when 13th Air Force notified 2d Air Division that a different target list was to be used. The 2d Air Division said it had the MACV target list and continued working on it. Shortly after, a phone call from PACAF indicated that JCS had changed the MACV target list and that 2d Air Division would hit target #14 [the Thanh Hoa railroad/highway bridge, aka the "Dragon's Jaw"], not #24 [the Chanh Hoa barracks SE and headquarters]. The 2d Air Division began working on the strike against Target #14 when information was received that Target #14 was scrubbed. Also, just before the F-105s were ready to deploy to Da Nang from Thai bases, word came in that they could strike from Thai bases. 2d Air Division was informed that the Navy would hit Target #24, VNAF Target #32 [the Vu Con barracks and supply depot] and the USAF would be limited to a flak/CAP [flak suppression/Combat Air Patrol] role. These last minute changes were difficult to assimilate, particularly where VNAF forces were involved. *PACAF subsequently told 2d Air Division that the changes, in practically all cases, stemmed from Washington-level with minimum lead time.* [Emphasis added]

During the strikes, overcast hindered accuracy, while flak destroyed five aircraft (the PAVN claimed 14). The next day, at McNamara's request, the JCS submitted a plan for American and Vietnamese airstrikes against barracks, bridges, depots, ferries and bases below the 19th Parallel, and armed reconnaissance along Route 7 near the Laotian border. Airmen would strike two to four targets per week over an eight-week period. Should the DRV's MiG-17s intervene, 30 B-52s from Andersen AFB on Guam would blitz Phuc Yen at night followed by 48 fighter-bombers at dawn. On February 13 Johnson announced a more restricted "program of measured and limited air action," noting "attacks might come about once or twice a week and involve two or three targets on each day of operation," to be called *Rolling Thunder*. On February 18, the JCS sent an "execute" order to PACOM for *Rolling Thunder I*, scheduled for February 20, against Quang Khe naval base and Vu Con barracks.

THE CAMPAIGN

"There ain't no daylight in Vietnam"

1965

Though scheduled for February 20, 1965, *Rolling Thunder I* missed its planned start date: and so did *Rolling Thunders II, III*, and *IV*. A convoluted demi-coup among South Vietnam's ever-contentious generals played out over several days, disrupting both the air campaign plan and unseating Nguyen Khanh little more than a year after he had seized power from "Big" Minh. In his place stepped the flamboyant Air Force chief, Nguyen Cao Ky, a lead-from-the-front A-1 pilot whose preferred dress was a natty all-black flight suit. Unlike the unfortunate Diem and Nhu, Khanh departed both alive and even with some face-saving decorum, being serenaded on his way by his erstwhile rivals, as Ambassador Maxwell Taylor looked on "glassily polite."

Rolling Thunder finally got underway on March 2, starting with *Rolling Thunder V*, without taking the North Vietnamese by surprise: two days earlier, on February 28, the American and South Vietnamese governments had issued a joint communiqué announcing the onset of "a continuous limited air campaign against the North to bring about a negotiated settlement on favorable terms." *Rolling Thunder V* sent some 160 Air Force and VNAF aircraft over the North against targets drawn from the Joint Chiefs' 94-target list compiled over six months previously. Supported by six KC-135 tankers, 25 F-100Ds, 20 F-105Ds, and 19 VNAF A-1Hs flew against the Quang Khe naval base (JCS Target 74), and 41 F-105Ds, 20 B-57Bs, and 12 F-100Ds struck an ammunition depot at Xóm Bang (JCS Target 64), with modest success.

But PAVN gunners shot down three F-105Ds, two F-100Ds, and one VNAF A-1H. The surprisingly high losses alarmed McNamara, who launched a top-level JCS review chaired by Deputy Secretary of Defense Cyrus Vance. His review, completed in mid-March, found that SEA loss rates so far were less than the Army Air Force experienced during World War II, though double Korea's. If the numbers were comforting, they were still ominous, given that they came at the beginning of an uncertain open-ended war, in an emerging era of smaller numbers of vastly more expensive airplanes; and that they reflected only flak and automatic weapons.

Flak downed this VA-15 Douglas A-4C Skyhawk (BuNo 149619) near Haiphong on October 4, 1967, while assigned to VA-15 off *Intrepid* (CVS-11). Pilot Lieutenant Commander Peter van Ruyter Schoeffel ejected safely, enduring more than five years of captivity. Here it is shown on April 24, 1965, being readied by the catapult crew for launch off the carrier *America* (CVA-66), when flying with VA-64. (NHHC)

Rolling Thunder VI, two days of Air Force–Navy–VNAF strikes, opened on March 14. That day, protected by USAF F-100Ds flying top cover and F-105Ds attacking antiaircraft sites, Nguyen Cao Ky personally led 24 VNAF A-1s – the only known historical case of a sitting head of state personally leading an air strike – against Tiger Island (JCS Target 39.16, known to the Vietnamese as Con Co Island), striking seven barracks with a mix of 250lb, 500lb, and 750lb bombs and inflicting roughly 70–80 percent damage. The next day, March 15, 64 A-1s and A-4s from *Hancock* (CVA-19) and *Ranger* (CVA-61), with 20 Air Force F-105Ds (and supported by 51 other USAF and USN aircraft) struck an ammo depot southwest of Phu Quý (JCS Target 40) with bombs, rockets, napalm (its first use over the North), and strafing. They damaged or destroyed 20 of 23 buildings, losing one A-1 and its pilot, and achieving only roughly 30 percent destruction. *Rolling Thunder VII*, a series of American and South Vietnamese strikes against various targets "decoupled" from any direct connection to Viet Cong provocations, followed over March 19–25. But already by then criticisms were growing.

Pessimism and constraints

Rolling Thunder was less than a week old when it drew its first barbs. In a phone conversation on March 6 with Senator Richard Russell (D-Ga), chair of the Senate Armed Services Committee, Johnson exclaimed "Airplanes ain't worth a *damn*, Dick!," reflecting his disappointment with *Rolling Thunder V*'s results. "A man can fight if he can see daylight down the road somewhere," he added morosely, concluding "But there ain't no daylight in Vietnam. There's not a bit." Russell replied with equal bitterness, "There's no end to the road. There's just nothing," adding "We're going to wind up with the people mad as hell with us."

These were surprisingly pessimistic sentiments, coming from a President who had just sent his airmen into war, and the US Senate's most powerful figure. Feeling that way, neither should have set in motion such an ill-considered air campaign, nor expanded US ground forces. On March 8, the first battalion-landing teams of the Marine's 9th Marine Expeditionary Brigade arrived at Da Nang, to protect this growing American air base, the brigade's mission statement naïvely directing that "The US Marine Force will not, repeat will not, engage in day-to-day actions against the Viet Cong." But of necessity, it was soon doing just that, the first steps into the SEA quagmire.

General Maxwell Taylor – Army Chief of Staff in the Eisenhower administration, and Chairman of the Joint Chiefs for Kennedy and Johnson – succeeded Henry Cabot Lodge as Ambassador to South Vietnam. (LBJL)

Criticism came as well from the newly appointed Ambassador in Saigon, Maxwell Taylor, still Johnson's *de facto* principal military confidant. "It appears to me evident that to date DRV leaders believe air strikes at present levels on their territory are meaningless and that we are more susceptible to international pressure for negotiations than are they," he scathingly wrote on March 8; "[we must] convince Hanoi authorities they face prospect of progressively severe punishment. I fear that to date *Rolling Thunder* in their eyes has been merely a few isolated thunderclaps." On March 13, he reiterated that Hanoi's leaders had "the impression that our air strikes are a limited attempt to improve our bargaining position and hence are no great cause for immediate concern" – an undisguised swipe at both George Ball's ill-considered essay and the joint US–South Vietnam communiqué, each of which revealed the boundaries of planned action – and urged that the Johnson administration "begin at once a progression of US strikes north of 19th Parallel in a slow but steadily ascending movement."

Taylor's recommendation for more northerly strikes highlighted a fundamental, growing, and never resolved conflict between the Defense Secretary and America's military professionals.

To McNamara, *Rolling Thunder* was never about North Vietnam *per se*. It was about the South: about coercing Hanoi's leaders to end their support of the Viet Cong. Doing so, he believed, required air attacks cutting supply lines to the Ho Chi Minh Trail. The air war might have to extend into the North above the DMZ, but only to support and bring victory to the South. "Neither the President, the Secretary of State, nor the Secretary of Defense yet conceived of *Rolling Thunder* as a strategic air offensive," Seventh Air Force's commander General William Momyer recalled after the war; "The Secretary of Defense continued to maintain that the primary role for air power should be to support ground forces in South Vietnam as it was here that the enemy must be denied a military victory." Thus, over 1965 through 1968, less than 30 percent of all 1,085,132 US attack sorties were "up North." Nearly 60 percent were in South Vietnam, and less than 20 percent were over Laos. (The numbers were 594,702 over South Vietnam, 306,618 over North Vietnam, and 183,812 over Laos.)

To professional airmen who had earned their spurs flying combat over North Africa, Europe, and Korea, this made no sense. Supplies arrived in North Vietnam through two major rail lines, the northwest and northeast, running down from China, and from the port of Haiphong,

Seventh Air Force Commander General William Momyer, a highly experienced air leader who was also an astute student of air power and aviation history disagreed strongly with how the Johnson administration was running of the air war. (USAF)

and were then sent south on roads and highways that repeatedly branched, becoming networks, then trails, then paths. Cutting individual nodes made as little sense as sopping up dripping water from an overflowing tub rather than turning off the tap. It meant risking scarce $2 million (in then-year dollars) jet fighters against $20,000 trucks, and, more likely still, against sandal-shod PAVN porters carrying A-frame loads. The logical targets were the traffic-dense ones – the railyards, bridges, roads, docks and port of Haiphong, petroleum storage, power, and airfields. It was just common-sense, hard-learned from military history.

But to Johnson, McNamara, and the oracular "Wise Men" they consulted, going further north risked war with China. They fundamentally misunderstood the complex dynamic between the DRV, the PRC, and the USSR, and the revolutionary zeal and both regional and global ambitions of party chairman Ho Chi Minh, general secretary Le Duan (Ho's more militant political rival and successor), and their associates. Typecasting North

Vietnam's leaders as pawns of Beijing rather than recognizing them for the strong-willed independent globally-minded revolutionaries they were, Johnson and McNamara assumed Mao was on a veritable hair-trigger, predisposed to leap at once to their assistance. Thus, all during *Rolling Thunder*, they fretted over a Korean War-like Chinese intervention. Even conceding the benefit of 20/20 hindsight, theirs was an unreasoning fear: about to plunge into the abyss of the Cultural Revolution, China faced a myriad of problems. The China delusion drove another, namely that they could persuade Soviet leaders to help broker peace between Hanoi, Saigon, and Washington. At the Manila war conference of October 1966 – when Soviet SA-2s, radars, MiGs, advisors, and technicians were flooding the DRV – Westmoreland listened in astonishment as Ambassador Averell

Viet Cong porters moving supplies along the Ho Chi Minh trail, 1965. (LC)

General William C. Westmoreland, MACV commander during *Rolling Thunder*, afterwards wrote he believed the policy of "graduated response" was "one of the most lamentable mistakes of the war." (LBJL)

Harriman, grandest of the State Department's legendary mandarins, earnestly asserted "The Russians are doing everything they can to bring peace in Vietnam."

Fear of Chinese intervention led to a 20–30-mile buffer zone, the so-called "China Strip," on top of two other circular restricted zones ringing Hanoi and Haiphong, which had a radius of 30 miles and 10 miles respectively. All three zones constrained maneuver, benefiting the North. Hanoi's and Haiphong's circles shielded supplies and MiGs and SAMs, while the China buffer, as General Charles "Chuck" Horner acidly recalled after *Desert Storm*, "worked wonderfully in Vietnam in terms of making us inefficient." It forced Air Force F-105 strikes from Thailand down a chute through the world's most heavily defended air space – Thud pilots and Wild Weasel electronic warfare officers dubbed it "Slaughter Alley" – infested with an estimated 150 SAM sites and thousands of antiaircraft weapons. Twice a day, Takhli- and Korat-based Thuds, capped by F-4s, ingressed from Laos, turning and racing southeast down a long 40-mile finger-like promontory north of Hanoi now known to history as Thud Ridge, flying lower than its ridgelines along its northern flank, whose escarpments and wooded hills masked them until they burst out from behind its solidity, turning south and "pushing it up" to meet the fury of the Red River Delta's air defenses.

Robert McNamara never budged from his determination to limit *Rolling Thunder*, always acted as a brake on expansion, defended doing so before Congress during contentious hearings in the mid-summer of 1967 and, after resigning as Secretary of Defense and leaving office in 1968, persisted in his views until his death, at age 93, in 2009. When new Air Force Chief of Staff General John McConnell, who had succeeded the legendary Curtis E. LeMay, proposed a LeMay-like plan for an intense 28-day campaign striking above the 19th and 20th Parallels, McNamara summarily rejected it. For a long time he also rejected various JCS proposals to attack "lucrative" targets including the DRV's petroleum storage and power plants – even once sending Chairman Wheeler and the Chiefs a rebuke for proposing such a "dangerous escalatory step" – until pressure from the Congress, the JCS, Lyndon Johnson, and the undeniably sorry pace of *Rolling Thunder* forced his hand in the summer and fall of 1967, just before he resigned.

"Target Tuesdays" and their consequences

Rolling Thunder's targeting reflected both Johnson and McNamara's extraordinarily strong personal desire to exert the tightest possible executive control. Indeed, working through his team and the Joint Chiefs, Johnson personally oversaw *Rolling Thunder* at the strategic, operational, and even tactical level, using the power of targeting as a means of exerting control. "I saw our bombs as my political resources for negotiating a peace," he boasted to biographer Doris Kearns, adding "By keeping a lid on all the designated targets, *I knew I could keep the control of the war in my own hands.*" [Emphasis added]

First, there was no approved campaign "plan," certainly not like Haywood Hansell's AWPD-1 before World War II, or the *Desert Storm* air campaign plan assembled at General Chuck Horner's direction by Brigadier General Buster Glosson and Lieutenant Colonel David Deptula, or even in the sense of a focused headquarters' think-piece like Colonel John Warden III's "Instant Thunder" response to Saddam Hussein's invasion of Kuwait. The closest was McConnell's 28-day, 94-target proposal, which the JCS had fleshed out into a four-phase concept for three weeks of strikes below the 20th Parallel on lines of communication, followed by a six-week campaign to cut the northeast and northwest rail lines into China, then a third phase of port, harbor, and mining strikes, and strikes on supply sites around Hanoi and Haiphong, and then a fourth phase essentially to hit anything else not already attacked, or incompletely so. But McNamara and Johnson would only approve more strikes against the lines of communications, only one out of many objectives the McConnell concept had originally addressed.

Instead folders on individual possible targets were assembled at PACOM (based on multiple sources of information); reviewed, winnowed down, and passed to the Pentagon's Joint Staff; reviewed and forwarded to the Joint Chiefs; reviewed again and then passed with recommendations to Secretary McNamara. He took them under advisement (typically running them past National Security Advisor McGeorge Bundy and Secretary of State Dean Rusk, and some of his own senior staff) and then passed them to Johnson with his recommendations. Johnson, meeting with all the principals, made final targeting decisions, usually doing so in lengthy Tuesday luncheons held at the White House and routinely attended by McNamara, McGeorge Bundy, Dean Rusk, and other administration civilian executives. Joint Chiefs Chairman General Earle Wheeler participated only by invitation, another measure of the gulf already separating senior military officials, the Johnson White House, and McNamara. Journalists joked about "Target Tuesdays," and CBS newsman Dan Rather reported on them in October 1967, calling McNamara "the man with the target list." "Field commanders are under instructions to not recommend [sic] certain targets in certain areas – Haiphong docks, the air defense command center in Hanoi, and so forth," Rather reported, adding (quite accurately) "There is much controversy and some bitterness about these off-limit targets."

Certainly, air commanders in the field – at PACOM's Pacific Air Forces (PACAF) and Pacific Fleet (PACFLT) in Hawaii; at Military Assistance Command Vietnam (MACV), the 2nd Air Division (2nd AD, which became the Seventh Air Force in 1966), and the 1st Marine Air Wing (1st MAW) in Vietnam; at the Seventh/Thirteenth Air Forces' headquarters in Thailand; or on Yankee and Dixie Stations with Task Force 77 (TF-77) – lacked the same freedom of planning, control, and execution that their predecessors had exercised in previous wars.

"On the eve of the April 1965 Honolulu Conference, Secretary McNamara still believed *Rolling Thunder* should be a limited application of air power against logistics targets relatively close to the Demilitarized Zone," Seventh Air Force's General William Momyer wrote, noting pointedly, "Further, the size and frequency of these strikes, as well as the targets, should be selected in Washington."

"Interference from Washington seriously hampered the campaign," MACV's General William Westmoreland recalled, noting that Lyndon Johnson bragged that airmen "can't even bomb an outhouse without my approval," and adding that "Washington had to approve all targets in North Vietnam, and even though the Joint Chiefs submitted long-range programs, the State Department constantly interfered with individual missions. This or that target was not to be hit for this or that nebulous non-military reason."

"I was never allowed in the early days to send a single airplane North [without being] told how many bombs I would have on it, how many airplanes were in the flight, and what time it would be over the target," 2nd Air Division's Major General Joseph H. Moore confirmed for service historians immediately after *Rolling Thunder*, noting "And if we couldn't get there at that time for some reason (weather or what not) we couldn't put the strike on later."

"One of the most aggravating [problems] was the frequently inordinate delay we experienced in receiving a reply from the JCS to proposals that required their

Johnson, McNamara, and the JCS discussing Vietnam at Johnson's ranch, December 22, 1964. Clockwise from top are General Curtis LeMay USAF (with trademark cigar), CJCS Earle Wheeler, Cyrus Vance, General Harold Johnson USA, Admiral David McDonald USN, General Wallace Green USMC (back to camera), LBJ, McNamara, and an unidentified colonel from the Joint Staff (far left). (LBJL)

OPPOSITE THE SOUTH EAST ASIA THEATER

approval," PACOM's Admiral Sharp recalled; "The reason was regrettably simple: the Chiefs could not get a decision from McNamara… [Later] instead of asking for permission to attack, we sent a message to the JCS saying that unless they indicated otherwise within 24 hours we would go ahead and strike… I am convinced it met with JCS approval because it forced the Secretary of Defense to make a timely decision if he wished to disapprove our plans."

No longer believing that he could, in good conscience, support Johnson's policy in Vietnam, John McCone, Director of the Central Intelligence Agency, took the extraordinary step of resigning less than two months after *Rolling Thunder* began: his was a principled action that the Joint Chiefs should have at least contemplated. As an air power advocate, the spy chief realized *Rolling Thunder*'s sporadic unstructured incrementalism could not possibly induce the DRV's leaders into abandoning their determined subversion of South Vietnam, Laos, and beyond, and he feared the alternative: a large investment of American forces deployed into the South.

"We must hit them harder, more frequently, and inflict greater damage," he wrote at the beginning of April 1965, in a final plea to McNamara, Rusk, Bundy, and Taylor: "We must change the ground rule of the strikes against North Vietnam. Instead of avoiding the MiGs, we must go in and take them out. A bridge here and there will not do the job. We must strike their air fields, their petroleum resources, power stations and the military compounds… promptly and with minimum restraint."

Only 20,389 soldiers, sailors, airmen, and Marines were serving in South Vietnam and Thailand when LBJ took office, this rising sharply to 103,812 by mid-1965. Then, in the wake of McCone's leaving, Johnson acceded to a request from Westmoreland on July 27, 1965 to deploy increased numbers of American troops – the first call was for 44 battalions – into Southeast Asia. By year's end American servicemen in theater had risen to 184,314, and this number would increase further, to 583,765 by the time Johnson announced he would not seek re-election in 1968.

Lieutenant General Joseph H. Moore, commander of the 2nd Air Division at the onset of *Rolling Thunder*, had a strong friendship with MACV commander Westmoreland rooted in their similar professional and social backgrounds. (USAF)

Johnson's national security team consistently underestimated Hanoi's commitment to the war; its steadily evolving technical, operational, and tactical competency; and the rapid pace of its military mobilization and expansion. By the end of 1965, North Vietnam had doubled the PAVN's army (as Merle Pribbenow has shown), from roughly 200,000 to 400,000, and sent 50,000 regulars down the Trail that year to fight in the South. (Americans first battled them in the four-day battle of Ia Drang Valley, the first major test of the Army's "Air Cavalry.")

Over that time, intelligence analysts and planners had added numerous "decimal targets" to the original JCS 94-target list, greatly complicating planning. Despite this, as PACOM's Sharp recalled, "We were still not permitted the latitude in the field, however, of preparing extended air campaign plans," adding, "The intent was obviously to keep any increase in the intensity of the air war firmly in the hands of the political decision-makers… The targets authorized for attack continued to be selected in Washington by the Secretary of Defense and the White House. Few of these were in the critical northeast quadrant, north of twenty degrees latitude, which contained the Hanoi/Haiphong military complexes and major port facilities, as well as the lines of communication to China."

In theater, airmen faced serious issues apportioning air power against the targets that were sent down from MACV, PACFLT, and PACAF. In the absence of a single air manager as existed later for *Desert Storm*, the 2nd Air Division and TF-77 had wisely established a *Rolling Thunder*

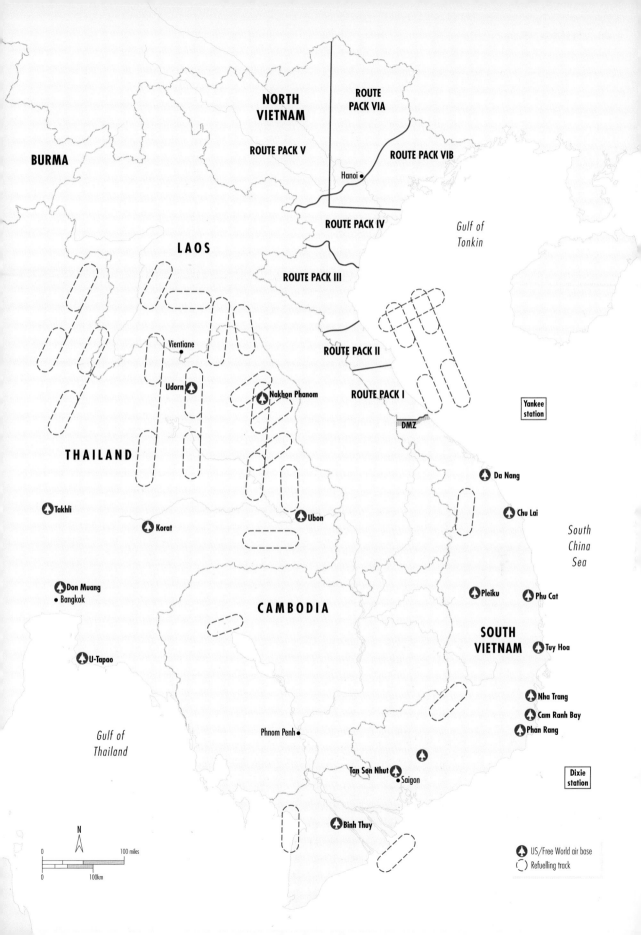

Coordination Committee. On its recommendation, on December 10, 1965, PACOM established an air power apportionment system across North Vietnam consisting of geographically defined Route Packages (RPs). Though well intended and seemingly logical, Route Packages constituted a compromise that artificially compartmentalized air power into little blocks, preventing unity of effort and unity of command. (They were deliberately rejected when advanced for *Desert Storm*.)

There were six "Route Packs" (RPs), from the demilitarized zone (DMZ) northwards to China and west to Laos. MACV had operational control over RP I, north of the DMZ, bounded in the east by Tonkin Gulf and in the west to the Laotian border; since this included the road network and passes feeding the Ho Chi Minh Trail, MACV coordinated its activities with the *Steel Tiger* and *Barrel Roll* interdiction operations over Laos. PACFLT had control of four coastal RPs, II, III, IV, and VI-A. RPs II, III, and IV together comprised an area bounded on the south by the northern border of RP I, on the west by Laos; on the east by the Tonkin Gulf, and on the north by a line along the 20° 31'N parallel from the Laotian border to Tonkin Gulf. PACAF had RP V bordering Laos in the west, China in the north, the 20° 31'N parallel in the south, and an eastern border running along the 105° 20'E longitude line from the 20° 31'N parallel due north to the Chinese border. RP VI included PACAF's RP VI-A, bounded to the west by RP V, to the north by China, and by a diagonal irregular border from 20° 31'N 105° 20'E northeast along the northeast rail line and Route 1A to the Chinese frontier; and PACFLT's RP VI-B, bounded to the south by the 20° 31'N parallel, to the southwest–northeast by the border of RP VI-B, to the north by China, and to the east by the Tonkin Gulf. To Southeast Asian airmen, "Pack Six," with the densely defended Hanoi and Haiphong, was no-explanation-necessary shorthand for the toughest, most heavily defended, most costly, air space over North Vietnam.

In 1964, Hanoi had lacked any air defense network worth considering. By late June 1965 that had changed, its gunners and MiG pilots having already inflicted significant losses – 50 aircraft (26 Navy, 24 Air Force) – highlighting the urgency of suppressing North Vietnam's growing air defense network. By the end of 1965 North Vietnam possessed an integrated air defense network, its essential elements netted together – radars, fighters, and surface-to-air missiles – so that taking it apart proved a formidable task: and one never fully realized.

The counter-radar war

Because Vietnam had not figured prominently in Western strategic air war planning, planners knew little about its radar defenses, except that they were growing at a rapid rate. Late in March 1965, concerned that North Vietnamese air defenders had better early warning than anticipated, PACOM initiated a series of strikes against known radar sites. Between March 22 and 31, Navy and Air Force strikes hit nine sites at Cap Mui Ron, Cua Lo, Dong Hoi, Ha Tinh, Vinh Linh, Vinh Son, and on Bach Long Vi, Hon Matt, and Hon Nieu islands, the start of an anti-radar campaign that grew exponentially more difficult over the next few months as the DRV, with Soviet assistance, introduced the SA-2, and undertook various deceptive measures, including setting up false signal emitters to lure strike aircraft into planned flak ambushes. DRV radar sites were heavily defended and thus extremely difficult to destroy. The first strike, against Vinh Son, cost a 67th Tactical Fighter Squadron (67th TFS) F-105D flown by squadron commander Lieutenant Colonel Robinson "Robbie" Risner – he was rescued by a Grumman HU-16B amphibian – and another on Bach Long Vi cost TF-77 six aircraft lost over two missions flown on March 26 and 29.

These early losses established a pattern illustrating why the counter-radar strikes were so important. In every analysis of combat aircraft losses over North Vietnam, ground fire – not MiGs or even SAMs – was always the predominant cause, and the ground fire, whether optically controlled or radar cued, was always radar dependent, if for no other reason than early warning.

SELECTED USAF COMBAT LOSSES OVER NORTH VIETNAM AND CAUSE[1]										
Type	Combat Loss Total	Cause								
		AAA		SA-2s		MiGs		Other		
		Number	Percent	Number	Percent	Number	Percent	Number	Percent	
F-4	193	127	65.80	24	12.43	37	19.17	5	2.60	
F-105	282	228	80.85	30	10.64	22	07.80	2	0.71	
RF-101	27	21	77.78	5	18.52	1	03.70	0	0	
RF-4	38	31	81.58	7	18.42	0	0	0	0	
Totals	540	407	75.37	66	12.22	60	11.11	7	01.30	
Notes 1 From: USAF, Comparative Analysis of USAF Fixed-Wing Aircraft Losses in SEA Combat, AFFDL-TR-77-115 (December 1977), Table A-1 (Part 1), p. 78.										

Looking across 540 combat losses over North Vietnam across the entire Vietnam War of four ubiquitous USAF "Pack Six" veterans – the F-105 and F-4 fighter-bombers and the RF-101 and RF-4 reconnaissance aircraft – AAA accounted for an average 75 percent of combat losses, with SAMs an average 12 percent, MiGs 11 percent, and "other" roughly 2 percent.

Over the period of *Rolling Thunder*, the workhorse F-105 – the campaign's iconic airplane – suffered 272 combat losses (over 36 percent of the total 753 F-105Ds and F-105Fs produced) over a total of 76,315 combat sorties, an average loss rate of 3.56 aircraft per 1,000 sorties. AAA accounted for almost 83 percent of all combat losses, with SA-2s slightly less than 10 percent and MiGs over 7 percent. But the averages can mask as well that at certain periods losses were much higher, particularly on certain missions.

Over the first 18 months of *Rolling Thunder*, F-105s flew 22,338 attack sorties over the North, sustaining 120 losses from flak, SAMs and MiGs, at a loss rate per 1,000 sorties of 5.37 airplanes. Over 52 days in July–August 1966, 25 Thuds were lost, 22 (88 percent) to AAA, two to SA-2s (8 percent), and one to a MiG (4 percent): an average of one Thud every two days – or, put another way, one Thud per Thud base (there were only two, Takhli and Korat) every four days. The F-105's record illustrates both the intensity of its air war deep in Pack VI, and also why some 60 percent of Thud pilots who set out to complete a 100-mission tour (as the late Thud pilot and historian Ed Rasimus computed) failed to do so.

THE F-105 OVER NORTH VIETNAM DURING ROLLING THUNDER, 1965–68[1]									
Year	Combat Loss Total	Cause of Combat Loss							
		AAA		SA-2s		MiGs		Combat Sorties/Loss Rate	
		No.	Percent	No.	Percent	No.	Percent	Combat Sorties	Loss Rate per 1,000 Sorties
1965	54	49	90.74	3	05.56	2	03.70	10,498	5.14
1966	102	94	92.16	5	04.90	3	02.94	24,602	4.15
1967	93	65	69.89	17	18.28	11	11.83	25,814	3.60
1968	23	17	73.91	2	08.70	4	17.39	15,401	1.49
Totals	272	225	82.72	27	09.93	20	07.35	76,315	3.56
Notes 1 From: USAF, Comparative Analysis of USAF Fixed-Wing Aircraft Losses in SEA Combat, AFFDL-TR-77-115 (December 1977), Table A-17 (Part 1), pp. 109–110.									

The war against North Vietnam's radar order of battle lasted throughout America's decade-long involvement in Southeast Asia, and took on even greater significance following the introduction of the SA-2 into combat in July 1965. Anticipating the introduction of the

OPPOSITE FIGHTER AIRFIELDS OF THE DRV AND RADAR DETECTION RANGES

SAM – a possibility then scoffed at by senior civilian defense officials in Washington, as discussed shortly – the Air Force deployed radar-locating Douglas RB-66Cs (redesignated EB-66C in the spring of 1966) to Southeast Asia in April 1965, the type completing its first radar mapping mission over the North on May 4. If lacking the allure of higher-performance strike aircraft, the RB/EB-66B/C (and the later EB-66E introduced in August 1967), like its EA-1F, EA-3B and EKA-3B naval stablemates and the Marine's venerable EF-10B and EA-6A, soon proved absolutely essential for aircrews venturing "Up North."

Taking on the MiGs

On April 1, 1965, ADF-VPAF commanders had met and decided to employ their MiG-17s in a veritable guerrilla air war, making sudden unexpected ground-controlled intercepts (GCI) on raiding American formations, and then withdrawing quickly. Two days later, they implemented this strategy, opening an air superiority war between American and North Vietnamese airmen and air defenders. During a Navy strike near Thanh Hoa, four 921st Regiment MiG-17s eluded an F-4B TARCAP from VF-151 off Coral Sea, bouncing four *Hancock* VF-211 F-8Es as they rocketed the Dong Phong Thong bridge. Though two MiG pilots each claimed an F-8 shot down, all the Crusaders survived, three trapping back on *Hancock*, and a fourth, badly shot up, diverting ashore to Da Nang. One MiG then ran out of fuel and landed on a river bank. (Since then, despite this mixed outcome, the DRV has celebrated April 3 as its Air Forces' Day.)

The next day, VPAF GCI controllers vectored four 921st MiG-17s behind four 354th TFS F-105Ds circling near Thanh Hoa preparing to attack the Ham Rong ("Dragon's Jaw") bridge (JCS Target 14). The leader and his wingman missed warnings, and both were shot down and killed. Afterwards, low on fuel, one MiG force-landed safely, but three did not: panicky flak or lack of fuel was most likely responsible, for no American airmen claimed them, although a 416th TFS F-100D pilot claimed a probable after hosing a diving MiG-17 that disappeared into a very low overcast over Tonkin Gulf, trailing bits of its right horizontal stabilizer and elevator.

Afterwards, in a telling study in contrasts, Ho Chi Minh congratulated his pilots while Lyndon Johnson (as the historian Jacob van Staaveren relates) informed the JCS that the "incident" was "unduly inflammatory," and "he did not want any more MiGs shot down" – as if that were something over which American airmen had total control.

Proving that point, just days later, on April 9, four VF-96 McDonnell F-4Bs off *Ranger* tangled in a confused dogfight with four Chinese PLAAF J-5s off Hainan Island during which the Phantoms fired 11 AIM-7 Sparrows and AIM-9 Sidewinders, claiming only a single J-5 destroyed, but at the price of a Phantom and its crew lost, to either an undetected MiG or an errant missile. The fight highlighted the uniformly poor performance of early Sidewinders and Sparrows, even when fired under optimum conditions (as some were); the mistake of having designed the F-4 – the most powerful and sophisticated fighter of its time – without a backup cannon armament; and the inherent risks maneuvering against the MiG-17/J-5 on its own terms.

In June and July, however, the big F-4B came into its own. On June 17, *Midway* VF-21 Phantom crews destroyed two MiGs – debris from the second victim claimed a third mortally damaged as well – with two impressive minimum-range "in your face" head-on AIM-7D Sparrow shots. Even propeller-driven Douglas A-1H Skyraiders improbably shared the limelight: on June 20, two *Midway* VA-25 A-1H pilots exhibiting remarkable cool-headedness and deadly marksmanship downed a MiG-17 that foolishly went beak-to-beak in an old-fashioned gun duel. (Subsequently, on October 9, 1966, an A-1H pilot of *Intrepid's* VA-176 cheekily bounced and bagged a Fresco.)

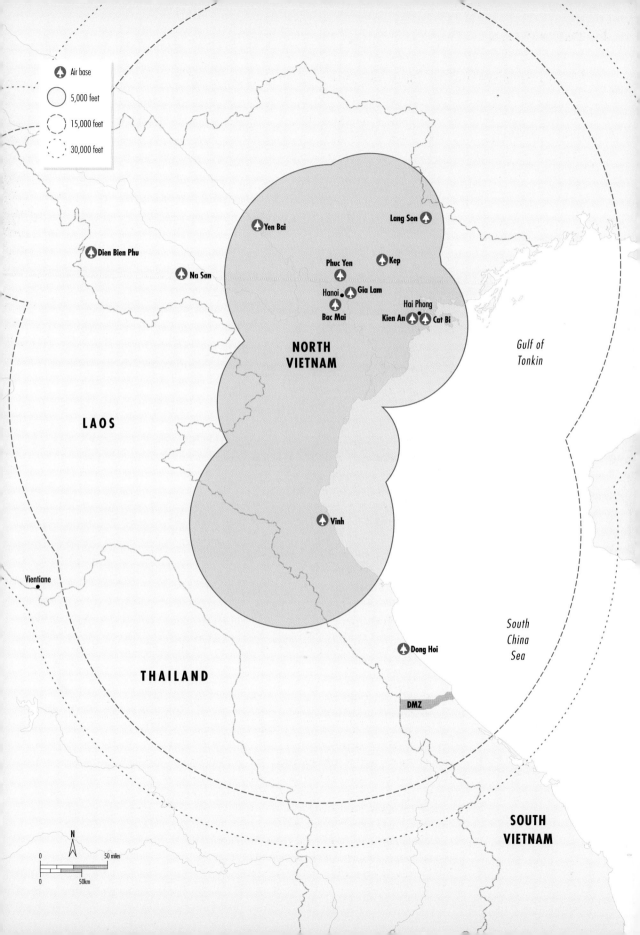

Air base

5,000 feet

15,000 feet

30,000 feet

Yen Bai

Lang Son

Dien Bien Phu

Na San

Phuc Yen

Kep

Hanoi

Gia Lam

Bac Mai

Hai Phong

Kien An

Cat Bi

NORTH VIETNAM

Gulf of Tonkin

LAOS

Vinh

Vientiane

South China Sea

THAILAND

Dong Hoi

DMZ

N

0   50 miles

0   50km

SOUTH VIETNAM

A gun camera catches the last seconds of a VPAF MiG-17, downed by Major Donald M. Russell of the 333rd TFS, using his Thud's 20mm Vulcan cannon, during a F-105 strike on the Dai Loi bridge (near Phuc Yen) on October 18, 1967. (NMUSAF)

For the US Air Force, the entry of MiGs into the air war triggered various deployments in April 1965: 18 F-4Cs of the 8th TFW's 45th TFS to Ubon RTAFB; five Lockheed EC-121D "Big Eye" airborne early warning and control aircraft of the 552nd AEWC Wing to Tan Son Nhut; and 14 Lockheed F-104Cs of the 476th TFS to Da Nang to protect the EC-121Ds. The 18-crew EC-121Ds, equipped with search and height-finder radars, began flying two 50 miles high-and-low racetrack patterns, Ethan Alpha and Ethan Bravo, over the Gulf of Tonkin, later adding a third, Ethan Charlie, over Laos in October 1966.

The EC-121D quickly proved its value: on July 10, 1965, a Big Eye crew detected two MiG-17s near Hanoi, warning two 45th TFS Phantom crews, who shot them both down. For the next nine months, the MiGs remained relatively quiescent, as North Vietnamese commanders concentrated on training pilots to survive encounters with hyper-aggressive American fighter pilots and avoiding "own goal" losses such as running out of fuel; they also trained flak gunners not to shoot down their own aircraft. Consequently, despite pressure from American field commanders and the JCS, Johnson and McNamara would not authorize attacking North Vietnam's fighter airfields at Kép and Hoa Lac until late April 1967, or Phuc Yen until late October 1967.

By then the fighter-versus-fighter air war had dramatically changed. In September 1965, the ADF-VPAF had formed a second MiG-17 regiment, the 923rd, at Kép. In January, its first MiG-21F-13 Fishbed entered service with the veteran 921st at Phuc Yen. In February 1966, the Central Intelligence Agency reported that North Vietnamese pilots were showing "a certain degree of increased aggressiveness," their "new-found confidence" likely a by-product of both better training and receiving their sleek new fighters. Comparative flight trials of a MiG-21 covertly acquired and exploited after *Rolling Thunder* confirmed that the MiG-17, because of its agility, always posed the greater threat, even though it had a poor gun system and gunsight. The early MiG-21, on the other hand, while dangerous to the unwary, had poor rearward visibility and low-altitude speed and structural limitations that greatly hindered it. Nevertheless, the Fishbed significantly influenced the air war, for it had a performance that matched the fastest American strike aircraft, was armed with heat-seeking Atoll air-to-air missiles based upon acquisition and exploitation of the early AIM-9 Sidewinder, and was small and difficult to see.

While Frescos remained the most dangerous and agile threat, the missile-armed Fishbed excelled at supersonic GCI-controlled hit-and-run passes through strike formations, firing a missile or two and then speeding off. Even if it didn't score, its presence often forced a strike package to jettison its ordnance and thus negate the mission. After a MiG-21 executed a nearly successful pop-up attack on a SAC Trojan Horse U-2 mission near Dien Bien Phu, further U-2 overflights were suspended. (The Mach 3.1 Lockheed A-12 Oxcart, single-seat precursor to the SR-71 Blackbird, began so-called "Black Shield" CIA-flown DRV overflights in March 1967, its performance guaranteeing invulnerability to early MiG-21s and most SA-2 engagement profiles.)

The Navy F-8, the Navy–Air Force F-4, and the Air Force F-105 all had high-end performance exceeding that of the MiG-17, and at least matching that of the MiG-21, and, if surprised, their defensive tactics called for taking the fight to lower altitudes, where the MiG-21's deficiencies were most pronounced. Generally speaking, the VPAF's dependence upon GCI tail-chase tactics worked against it for, if warned by Air Force EC-121s or Navy E-1s of impending attack and having sufficient range separation, a supersonic fighter or strike aircraft like the F-105, F-4, or F-8 could turn into the attacker, forcing an abort. It was crucial to keep a high airspeed – at least Mach 1.1 and preferably more – and avoid trying to out-turn or out-climb either the Fresco or the Fishbed. For Thuds, a hard, slightly descending afterburner turn into approaching MiGs generated rapid separation, followed by a nose-down accelerating withdrawal to lower altitudes where its extraordinary speed frustrated any adversary. For their part, the MiG pilots had learned that they, too, could use the agility of their aircraft to frustrate American fighters, and the troubled missiles that they fired.

On January 2, 1967, Colonel Robin Olds' 8th TFW fully exploited the performance and weapons advantage of the F-4 against the VPAF's Fishbeds. In Operation *Bolo*, the war's best-known dogfight, the "Wolfpack's" Phantom crews used deception – mimicking an ingressing F-105 flight in all respects, including use of Thud jamming pods – to lure the MiGs into combat, destroying seven MiG-21s in 12 minutes. Afterwards the battered 921st Fighter Regiment stood down for several months to recover, not returning to combat until April, employing larger formations and a mix of tactics, including flying at low level to evade F-4 radars, popping up behind formations, and diving in pairs through them on a Mach 1.3 single missile-firing pass. To counter strikes from Thailand, the Fishbed fliers established two orbits, one 35 miles northwest of Phuc Yen air base, and the other 35 miles southwest of it, with a third just slightly south of Phuc Yen in case a strike came in from Tonkin Gulf. Older MiG-17s assumed wheel formations, hoping to lure more heavily wing-loaded American fighters into energy-depleting turning fights, though generally without success.

The VPAF's new tactics, coupled with better pilot discipline, worked well. Over the first half of 1967, American fighter aircrews had shot down 54 MiGs for 11 lost, a relatively good exchange rate, though not as good as that of their predecessors in

Two Raytheon AIM-9B Sidewinders on an F-105D c. 1965; far more typically, F-105Ds flew with a single AIM-9B on one outer wing pylon, and an ECM pod on the opposite outer pylon. (NMUSAF)

World War II or Korea. In January, they had even downed nine MiGs (including Operation *Bolo*'s seven) for no losses at all. But in April, though shooting down another nine MiGs, they lost seven of their own, a disturbing 1.3 to 1 exchange rate. In May, the Air Force and Navy had a good month – it went into the books as the "May Massacre" – downing 26 MiGs for the loss of two F-4Cs. The month included a notable Navy fur-ball on May 19 covering a Walleye-tossing two-ship *Bonnie Dick* VA-212 A-4 strike on Hanoi's thermal power plant. Amidst a dense barrage of SAMs and flak, the A-4s hit the plant, while four MiG-17s fell to angry F-8Es, two apiece shot down by VF-24 and VF-211 'Sader drivers. But two F-8s were lost, one to an SA-2 and one to flak, dampening any celebrations. In subsequent encounters, MiG pilots showed heightened cooperation, one flight seeking to lure any MiGCAP away so another could attack the bombers, whether Air Force F-105s, Navy A-4s, or the newer high-wing Navy Vought A-7 Corsair II (resembling a stubby F-8, and introduced to the war in early December 1967 by *Ranger*'s VA-147). In the last two months of the year, the VPAF lost six MiG-17s – but shot down four F-105s and five F-4s (three USAF F-4Ds and two Navy F-4Bs), for a 1.5 to 1 exchange rate favoring DRV airmen.

The MiGs' new-found success might well have reflected another development. In September 1966, the North Vietnamese and North Korean General Staffs reached agreement for North Korean exchange pilots to fly combat in DRV MiGs. A North Korean detachment numbering slightly less than 90 airmen, designated "Doan Z" ("Delegation Z"), subsequently flew MiG-17s out of Kép from the summer of 1967 to 1969. Whatever success Doan Z later enjoyed came only after a steep and costly learning curve: on July 21, 1967, for example, four of its airmen fell (three perishing) before the Sidewinders and 20mm cannon of marauding F-8C and F-8E pilots of *Bon Homme Richard*'s VF-24 and VF-211, screening *"Bonnie Dick"* A-4s bombing a POL storage site at Ta Xa. Overall, Doan Z eventually lost 14 of its personnel, while improbably claiming 26 American airplanes. Until Hanoi's or Pyongyang's archivists release further information, Doan Z's contributions to the DRV's air defense will remain a tantalizing speculation.

By the time Lyndon Johnson restricted *Rolling Thunder* and announced he would not run for re-election, the VPAF fighter force numbered approximately 118 aircraft, 100 of which were in sanctuary on Chinese airfields. In the first two months of 1968 VPAF MiGs shot down ten American aircraft for the loss of nine, and were sighted flying in Route Pack III and IV. Even as SAM effectiveness declined – now taking upwards of 65 missiles to kill a single aircraft – MiG successes rose alarmingly: from accounting for just 1 percent of US aircraft losses in 1965, to 3 percent in 1966, 8 percent in 1967, and a whopping 22 percent in the first quarter of 1968.

In at least four cases from June through September 1968, Marine EA-6A, Navy EKA-3B, and Air Force EB-66E jamming crucially assisted four MiG shoot-downs by Navy pilots and missileers for, in addition to attacking North Vietnam's radar order of battle, the electron-slingers could jam GCI and VPAF fighter communications, leaving MiGs deafened, isolated, and bereft of warning. On June 26, EA-6A comm jamming led to a MiG-21 being shot down by a VF-51 F-8H; on July 9, EA-6A and EKA-3B jamming blocked warnings to a wandering MiG-17 subsequently shot down by a VF-191 F-8E; on July 10, EA-6A and EKA-3B jamming left two MiG-21s unaware of nearby VF-33 F-4Js, resulting in one Fishbed lost; finally, on September 22, EB-66E and EA-6A jamming resulted in a MiG-21 being downed over North Vietnam's panhandle by a RIM-8 Talos ramjet-powered SAM fired from the guided missile cruiser USS *Long Beach* (CGN-9); this was its second Talos victory (the first had been on May 23) and, as it was an *American* SAM versus a *Vietnamese* fighter, a bit of a "man bites dog" tale as well.

The table below summarizes *Rolling Thunder*'s fighter-versus-fighter air war over the North, and the relative contributions of the various Air Force and Navy fighter aircraft involved.

VPAF LOSSES BY US TYPE AND SERVICE, 1965–68										
Year	Type Lost	USAF Type Credited		USN Type Credited					VPAF Losses by Year & Type	
		F-4[1]	F-105	A-1	A-4	F-4[2]	F-8	Talos[3]		
1965	MiG-17[4]	2	-	1	-	4	-	-	MiG-17	7
	MiG-21	-	-	-	-	-	-	-	MiG-21	0
	An-2[5]	-	-	-	-	-	-	-	An-2	0
1966	MiG-17	7	5	1	-	1	3	-	MiG-17	17
	MiG-21	5	-	-	-	-	1	-	MiG-21	6
	An-2	-	-	-	-	2	-	-	An-2	2
1967	MiG-17	19.5	21.5	-	1	2	9	-	MiG-17	53
	MiG-21	17	-	-	-	3	-	-	MiG-21	20
	An-2	-	-	-	-	-	-	-	An-2	0
1968	MiG-17	5	-	-	-	-	2	-	MiG-17	7
	MiG-21	3	-	-	-	2	3	2	MiG-21	10
	An-2	-	-	-	-	-	-	-	An-2	0
US Credits		F-4[1]	F-105	A-1	A-4	F-4[2]	F-8	Talos	Total Credits	
		58.5	26.5	2	1	14	18	2	122	
VPAF Type	MiG-17	33.5	26.5	2	1	7	14	-	84	
	MiG-21	25	-	-	-	5	4	2	36	
	An-2	-	-	-	-	2	-	-	2	
US Credits by Branch of Service		USAF: 85					USN: 37			

Notes
1 USAF F-4C or F-4D.
2 USN F-4B or F-4J.
3 Shipboard surface-to-air missile; rocket-boosted, but ramjet-sustained.
4 1965 MiG-17s lost include one fatally hit by debris from a MiG blown up by an AIM-7, on 17 June 1965.
5 Light biplane transport used by the VPAF for special operations insertions into Laos.

Confounding the SA-2

Over the spring and summer of 1965 another threat – one disturbingly ignored – emerged to radically transform the air superiority war and combat operations over the North generally: the Soviet Vympel S-75 (SA-2) surface-to-air missile. If American fighter pilots generally looked forward to tangling with MiGs, SAMs were a very different matter: fast, implacable, not subject to fear or intimidation, and utterly deadly.

On April 5, both a high-altitude Air Force Lockheed U-2D from the 4028th SRS flying a Trojan Horse strategic reconnaissance mission out of Bien Hoa and a low-altitude *Coral Sea* RF-8A recce Crusader from VFP-63 Detachment (Det) D, photographed a SA-2 site under construction 15 miles southeast of Hanoi. When briefed in Saigon both by MACV's Westmoreland and by 2nd Air Division's Moore on the danger posed by the SA-2 – and the necessity of immediately bombing the sites – John McNaughton, Assistant Secretary of Defense for International Security Affairs, and a man who prided himself on his analytical and quantitative skills, reacted with astonishment, even ridicule. "You don't think the North Vietnamese are going to use them?" he exclaimed to Moore, adding with some condescension "Putting them in is just a political ploy by the Russians to appease Hanoi." To Westmoreland, it was a shocking and revelatory moment. "'It was all a matter of signals,' said the clever civilian theorists in Washington," he wrote mockingly; 'We won't bomb the SAM sites, which signals the North Vietnamese not to use them.' Had it not been so serious, it would have been amusing."

The Joint Chiefs wisely thought otherwise and recommended bombing this and other emerging sites. But on May 6, 1965, McNamara rejected doing so, fearing that possible Soviet casualties might lead to a widening of the war. North Vietnam's SAM build-up

MISSILE

MISSILE

CAMOUFLAGE NET

RADAR

CABLE CROSSING

MISSILE

MISSILE

MISSILE TRANSPORTER
POSITIONING BLOCKS

WOOD OR BAMBOO MATTING

A North Vietnamese S-75 Dvina (NATO SA-2 Guideline) site, photographed in 1965. Note the centrally located SNR-75 (NATO Fan Song) radar. (USIA via NHHC).

thus continued uninterrupted, McNaughton's and McNamara's actions exemplifying the astonishing detachment of Washington's political class from the threats and sobering realities of Southeast Asian combat.

By the time McNaughton blew up at Moore, the DRV was well along towards fielding the SA-2, the Ministry of Defense having issued Decision 03/QD-QP, forming the PAVN's first SAM unit (the 236th Missile Regiment) on January 7, 1965. Under military commander Nguyen Quang Tuyen and political commissar Pham Dang Ty, the 236th depended during much of its first year on visiting Soviet technical advisors for its operational capability and expertise. (In April 1965, PVO-Strany deployed 70 SAM experts to North Vietnam – the first of approximately 3,000 PVO-Strany personnel sent to North Vietnam over *Rolling Thunder*, a dozen or so of whom were killed in action; not until August 24, 1965 would an all-PAVN SAM crew fire a SA-2 in anger.)

By May, the first of nearly 8,000 Vympel S-75 SAMs had arrived in the DRV, and the 236th Regiment had begun training in earnest. Hundreds of scientific and technical faculty and students were brought from polytechnics and technical schools to staff the expanding air defense program. Three SAM training and support sites in Ha Tay province in the Red River Delta were supporting the emerging SAM force: one for the 236th; a second for the 238th (established on April 22 and likewise working up under Soviet tutelage); and a third training site commanders and missile operators and maintainers on newly acquired P-35 Saturn (NATO Bar Lock) and P-12 Yenisei (NATO Spoon Rest) EW/GCI radars, and the PRV-11 (NATO Side Net) height-finding radar, the latter typically paired with the P-15 Trail (NATO Flat Face A) EW radar.

As North Vietnam prepared for battle, on May 13, the Johnson administration began a unilateral bombing pause, suspending all *Rolling Thunder* strikes. But this proffered carrot failed to stimulate any sort of favorable DRV response and so, on May 18, the pause ended, and bombing resumed. On May 19, the air defense command established a Hanoi Air Defense Regional Headquarters headed by military commander Nguyen Duong Han and political commissar Tran Van Giang and a Haiphong Air Defense Regional Headquarters under military commander Nguyen Huu Ich and political commissar Luong Ti. That same month, DRV Vice-Premier Le Thanh Nghi ordered expansion of airfields at Hoa Lac, Kép, Tho Xuan, and Yen Bai; the rebuilding of Gia Lam and Kien An; and installation of GCI stations at Kien An, Tho Xuan, and Vinh airfields.

On July 18, ADF-VPAF headquarters ordered two batteries – the 63rd and 64th – of the 236th Missile Regiment relocated northwest from Hanoi to Trung Ha near Son Tay. There they would be joined by two conventional AA regiments from the 361st AA Division, and a radar company from the 291st Radar Regiment with a Knife Rest-B EW radar. The move was made in hopes that doing so would create an ambush trap: first the missiles would have their shot, then the launchers would be moved and replaced with dummies, affording the conventional AA troops their own opportunity to down more aircraft on any retaliatory mission.

On the morning of July 24 an RB-66C mission detected Fan Song radar signals from two heretofore undetected SA-2 sites, fixing their position and passing the coordinates to higher headquarters. Early that afternoon, an ingressing Thud pilot heard "bluebells ringing, bluebells ringing!" – the prearranged SAM launch warning – then saw the flaring boosters of rising SA-2s. "I could not see what the target was," he recalled, "but all hell broke out shortly thereafter."

Fired by a PVO-Strany team, the SAMs homed undetected on Leopard Flight, four F-4C Phantom IIs of the 47th TFS, flying northwest of Hoa Binh 13,000ft above the cloud deck. One detonated close under the formation, its fragments impacting all four Phantoms, and leaving one a flaming, tumbling wreck. Its pilot ejected and was taken prisoner, but shrapnel mortally wounded his backseater – a fighter pilot serving as a weapon systems officer.

As planned, that night the two SAM battalions swiftly relocated. On the 26th, Johnson met with his national security team: the JCS wanted to destroy all seven SAM sites then in the north; JCS Chairman Wheeler recommended three (Sites 4, 6, and 7), but McNamara cleared just two (Sites 6 and 7), dropping the third (Site 4) because attacking it "would vex the Soviets." Quite reasonably, Vice President Hubert Humphery asked might the missiles already have been moved. "We are over-estimating the mobility of these units," McNamara tartly replied in smug ignorance. Press secretary Jack Valenti opined somewhat absently "This could be a piece of definitive action that would signal our determination." Sensing useful conversation at an end, Johnson then ordered emphatically "TAKE THEM OUT." Just hours later, on July 27, 46 Takhli and Korat F-105Ds attacking from as low as 50ft flew into a hornet's nest of 57mm and 37mm antiaircraft fire, losing six aircraft (four to flak, and a shot-up fifth which fatally collided with an undamaged sixth), with three pilots killed, two captured, and only one rescued.

"The [anti-SAM] mission was just stupid," recalled Chuck Horner, who, as a young captain, had flown on it; "I concluded at the time that low-level attack was a loser." *Rolling Thunder* convinced him that "air war planning was being done by people far away from the theater of operations who had no appreciation for the realities," and that "a bunch of amateurs were running things." The memory of that shaped the way he would structure the *Desert Storm* air campaign plan a quarter-century later.

ABOVE The Air Force combat search and rescue (CSAR) all-stars, flying along the Mekong near Nakhon Phanom in April 1968: a Lockheed HC-130P of the 40th Aerospace Rescue and Recovery Squadron (40th ARRS) refuels a Sikorsky HH-3E Jolly Green Giant of the 37th ARRS, while escorted by two Douglas A-1E and 2 A-1H Sandys of the 602nd Special Operations Squadron (602nd SOS). (NMUSAF)

LEFT In a war with many extraordinary "saves," arguably the rescue of RF-8G pilot Lieutenant Commander Tom Tucker from Haiphong's ship-jammed inner harbor – plucked by HS-6 CO Commander Bob Vermilya's doggedly courageous Sikorsky SH-3A Sea King crew on August 31, 1966 – was the most incredible: they survived over 20 minutes of continuous gunfire without taking a hit. (NHHC)

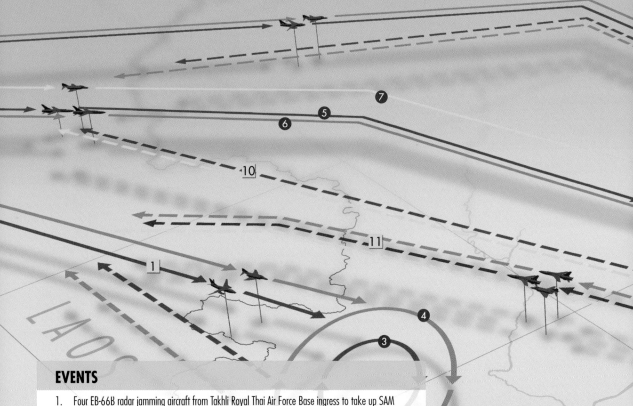

EVENTS

1. Four EB-66B radar jamming aircraft from Takhli Royal Thai Air Force Base ingress to take up SAM jamming positions over northern and central North Vietnam. Sweeping ahead of each pair is a flight of four F-4Cs based at Ubon Royal Thai Air Force Base.

2. The strike package of 16 F-105Ds, protected by F-105F Wild Weasels and F-4Cs, heads for the Thai Nguyen industrial complex, one of two Alpha strike packages that will attack Thai Nguyen on this day. The strike package descends to 9,500ft and accelerates to 550 knots to minimize risk of losses to BARLOCK-guided MiG-21s.

3. Vietnamese SAM sites are alerted to an incoming raid. Three Shenyang J-5s from Yen Bai shadow the ingressing EB-66 jammer, then engage the F-4C MiG CAP; the lead J-5 is shot down. The two remaining then fly south of Phuc Yen, and engage the F-105D strike package, before returning to land at Yen Bai.

4. The F-105D strike package, at 480 knots, turns on jamming pods, and Flight leads ensure proper spacing between flights for mutual jamming protection. The MiG CAP follows the Weasels to prevent MiG pop-ups and stern shots.

5. The northern EB-66s begin their jamming, targeting the Bac Mai and Phuc Yen (Noi Bai) GCI posts.

6. Two MiG-17Fs from Kep attempt to shoot down the EB-66 jammer (which is seriously hampering communications and the VPAF's air defense order of battle) but the F-4 CAP wards them off. They return to Kep.

7. The F-105D strike package turns parallel to Thud Ridge, jinking and weaving to defeat AAA, maintaining formation to ensure optimum jammer protection.

8. Two VPAF MiG-21F-13s from Phuc Yen cross Thud Ridge, attempt (and fail) to close with the F-105D strike package , then circle Kep before returning to Phuc Yen.

9. The F-105D strike package attacks Thai Nguyen, releasing bombs and executing 4g pullouts to remain above 4,500ft (beyond light weapons and small-arms range).

10. 57mm AAA seriously damages one F-105D; accompanied by an F-4 element, its pilot makes for Laos, where he is forced to eject.

11. All US aircraft egress into Laotian airspace, refuel on the Green Anchor Extend track, and return to their respective bases.

UNITED STATES AIR FORCE UNITS ●

EB-66 Jammers and MIG CAP:
1. 2 x EB-66B radar jamming aircraft (41st TEWS, 355th TFW)
2. A Flight (4x F-4C) (433rd TFS, 8th TFW)
3. 1x EB-66C radar jamming aircraft (41st TEWS, 355th TFW)
4. B Flight (4x F-4C) (433rd TFS, 8th TFW)

Strike Package, Strike Protection, and MIG CAP:
5. 16x F-105D (A, B, C, D flights) (354th TFS, 355th TFW). Armed with M-117 bombs.
6. 8x F-105F Wild Weasels (E and F flights) (333rd TFS). E Flt armed with 2 AGM-45 Shrike ARMs and 2 CBU-24 cluster bombs for SAM suppression. F Flt armed with 2 AGM-45 Shrike ARMS and two SUU-30 chaff dispensers.
7. 16x F-4C, MIG CAP (4 flights – A, B, C and D– of four aircraft) (555th TFS, 8th TFW). Armed with 4 AIM-7 and 4 AIM-9.

VIETNAM PEOPLE'S AIR FORCE ● UNITS

A. Three Shenyang J-5s (MiG-17F, NATO Fresco-A), 923rd Fighter Regiment (Yen Bai)
B. Two MiG-21F-13s (NATO Fishbed-C], 921st Fighter Regiment (Phuc Yen), each armed with 2 Vympel R-3S (K-13) [NATO Atoll] IR AAMs
C. Two MiG-17Fs, 923rd Fighter Regiment (Kep)

Air Force F-105 Alpha Strike Package into Route Pack VIA against Thai Nguyen
1967

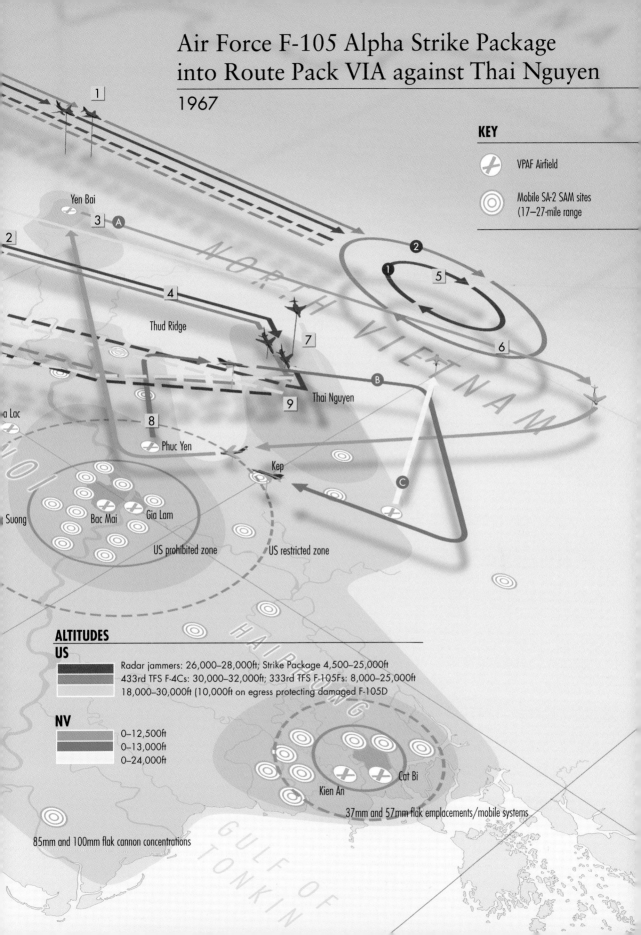

KEY

VPAF Airfield

Mobile SA-2 SAM sites (17–27-mile range

Yen Bai

NORTH VIETNAM

Thud Ridge

Thai Nguyen

a Lac

Phuc Yen

Kep

Suong

Bac Mai

Gia Lam

US prohibited zone

US restricted zone

HAIPHONG

ALTITUDES

US

Radar jammers: 26,000–28,000ft; Strike Package 4,500–25,000ft
433rd TFS F-4Cs: 30,000–32,000ft; 333rd TFS F-105Fs: 8,000–25,000ft
18,000–30,000ft (10,000ft on egress protecting damaged F-105D

NV

0–12,500ft
0–13,000ft
0–24,000ft

37mm and 57mm flak emplacements/mobile systems

Kien An

Cat Bi

85mm and 100mm flak cannon concentrations

GULF OF TONKIN

Air Force, Navy, and Marine airborne jammers were crucial to executing a successful strike. Here is a Douglas EB-66E Destroyer (SN 54-440) of the 42nd Tactical Electronic Warfare Squadron (42nd TEWS), 355th TFW, based at Takhli RTAFB in 1968. The EB-66 force jammed Fire Can, Bar Lock, Spoon Rest, and Fan Song radars, saving many strikers operating in Route Packs VI-A and VI-B.

There was one bright spot: the rescue of 12th TFS Thud pilot Captain Frank Tullo by a bold Sikorsky CH-3C crew, Shed 85, skippered by Captain George Martin. In an unarmed – and unarmored – cargo helicopter (unlike later armored and armed HH-3s and HH-53s) possessing only a jury-rigged rescue hoist and plagued by over-temping engines, they flew deep into North Vietnam, even landing in a dry rice paddy so Tullo could scramble aboard! Two A-1Hs from *Midway's* VA-25 and two of Tullo's fellow Thud pilots strafed approaching PAVN troops, keeping both rescuers and rescued from further harm. All throughout *Rolling Thunder*, the Air Force and Navy air rescue crews routinely displayed bravery, dedication, and steadfastness that earned them a unique privilege – rarely, if ever, having to pay for their own drinks when around any aircrew who flew Up North.

The PAVN established another ambush cluster well to the south of Hanoi and on the night of August 11–12, it caught the pilots of two Douglas A-4E Skyhawks from VA-23 off *Midway* out on a road recce mission. They saw two lights wobbling below them, realizing too late that they were homing SA-2s. The missiles seriously damaged both aircraft. Fortunately, they reached Tonkin Gulf, the wingman ejecting and being rescued by a destroyer, while the flight leader trapped safely aboard the *Midway.*

Like the Air Force after the July 24 shootdown, TF-77 launched a series of missions on August 13 to find the launch site, but by then it had moved, replaced (as earlier) with dummy equipment screened by the 230th AA Regiment. By day's end, TF-77 had lost five aircraft and two pilots, with seven others damaged. Afterwards, perhaps mindful of their cost, Ho Chi Minh exhorted the PAVN's missileers to "shoot down more airplanes with fewer missiles."

These two experiences, one Air Force, one Navy, forced immediate emphasis on signals intelligence, jamming, and counter-SAM tactics and attack, subjects which the United States had devoted too little attention before the war. (Not until 1968, for example, would the Air Force issue a tactics manual for its EB-66). Largely learning "on the job," Air Force, Navy, and Marine crews of R/EB-66B/C/E Destroyer, EA-1F Skyraider, EA-3B (and later EKA-3B) Skywarrior, EF-10B Skyknight, and Grumman EA-6A Intruder EW aircraft waged a complex technical war against North Vietnam's increasingly diverse and sophisticated radar order of battle.

Not often receiving due credit are the naval and Marine aviators who flew the propeller-driven EA-1F (formerly AD-5Q) of VAW-13 (later VAQ-130) and VAW-33 (later VAQ-33), and the aging, woefully underpowered twin-jet EF-10Bs (formerly F3D-2Q, an EW derivative of the MiG-15-killing F3D-2 nightfighter) of VMCJ-1. Until the radar-jamming EB-66B arrived at Takhli in October 1965, the EA-1F and EF-10B executed most jamming, for the RB-66C, like the Navy's EA-3B (formerly A3D-2Q), was primarily a signals gatherer and warner.

Though soon prudently withdrawn from North Vietnamese skies, the EA-1F and EF-10B did yeoman service in the early months of *Rolling Thunder*. EA-1Fs flew jamming missions off North Vietnam, occasionally venturing over the coast as air rescue coordinators. VMCJ-1 EF-10Bs orbited over Tonkin Gulf and ventured into North Vietnam to support Air Force and Navy strikes, logging over 9,000 combat sorties in three years, and losing two aircraft and their crews to enemy fire, before being replaced by the much more capable "Electric Intruder," the EA-6A.

The faster, more powerful, and larger twin-engine EB-66B/Es, EKA-3B (a jammer-tanker A-3B derivative that flew in the last year of *Rolling Thunder*) and new EA-6A, all air-refuellable, had stronger and more diverse jamming capabilities than the piston engine EA-1F and EF-10B. The first Air Force EB-66B jammers arrived at Takhli in October 1965. The EB-66B worked in concert with EB-66Cs, emitting a noise barrage against Whiff, Fire Can, and Fan Song radars. Initially the EB-66s flew deep into North Vietnam, but following the shootdown of an EB-66C by a SAM near Vinh in February 1966, EB-66 orbits moved further west, and further still when, later in 1966, the ADF-VPAF moved SA-2 batteries into northwest North Vietnam. By the summer of 1967, the introduction of MiG-21s and extension of MiG operations had forced an even further distancing of EB-66 operations to below the 20th Parallel, reducing the effectiveness of barrage jamming directed at radars in the Red River Delta, the heart of "Pack Six," and the jamming of VPAF MiG IFF (Identification Friend or Foe) signals. In October 1967, following changes in equipment and redeployment of North Vietnamese SAM defenses to protect Hanoi and Haiphong, EB-66 orbits moved back into the North, though, unfortunately, this led to an EB-66C being lost to a MiG-21 in January 1968, resulting in Seventh Air Force forbidding all EB-66 operations over North Vietnam for the remainder of *Rolling Thunder*. Instead, they orbited over Tonkin Gulf or Laos. Working in concert, an EB-66E (an upgraded EB-66B whose jammers could be tuned in flight) over Laos and another over Tonkin Gulf could jam radars so efficiently that the ADF-VPAF would be unaware of approaching aircraft until they were as close as 10–30nm to their targets.

Iron Hand and Wild Weasels

While jamming greatly improved mission safety, on its own it could not defeat the SAM threat. What was also needed was a "hard kill" capability – finding, fixing, targeting, and then physically destroying SAM sites, even, if possible, as strike operations were underway. As the Air Force's and Navy's first reaction strikes showed, this was far from easy. There were alternatives, such as using Ryan BQM-34 reconnaissance drones launched by Lockheed DC-130As out of Bien Hoa to lure SAM sites into giving away their positions, to then be attacked by a standby flight of armed F-105Ds on alert; but these were disappointing, often resulting in additional losses as airmen hunted over dense antiaircraft concentrations looking for SAM sites. Even veteran airmen were not immune: on February 16, 1966, Lieutenant Colonel Robbie Risner was shot down skimming less than 100ft above a hill-crest, subsequently enduring over seven years as a POW.

A better approach was to use modified fighter and attack aircraft which could keep up with a strike flight and penetrate to the target area. Out of this grew Iron Hand, so-named by Captain Alton B. Grimes, a former *Ranger* skipper on the Pentagon's reconnaissance staff, established on August 12, 1965. Strike aircraft equipped with defensive electronic countermeasures and radar location receivers would attack SAM sites, typically employing a new Navy-developed radar-homing missile, the Texas Instruments AGM-45 Shrike. An outgrowth of the Sparrow, the Shrike gave SAM-hunters a lethal punch, but still with some limitations, notably small warhead size, lack of homing "memory" if a radar shut down (thus rendering it "stupid"), and roughly half the SA-2's 17-mile effective range and speed. Later, Major Leo Thorsness and electronic warfare officer (EWO) Captain Harry Johnson conceived the "Shrike toss:" burner-climb an F-105F to 35,000ft, hold 45-degree nose-up, and fire a Shrike, killing Fan Songs up to 35 miles distant.

On October 17, 1965, a VA-75 Grumman A-6A led four VA-72 A-4Es that bombed a SAM site operated by the 82nd Battalion of the 238th Missile Regiment, destroying several of its launchers, its Fan Song radar, and other equipment. (In early 1968, in time for the last few months of *Rolling Thunder*, the Navy introduced the A-6B into the fleet, a dedicated SAM-killer armed with Shrikes and the longer-range and more capable AGM-78 Standard ARM, beginning with three deployed with VA-75 aboard *Kitty Hawk*.) The Navy used as well VQ-1 EA-3Bs to search for Fan Song signals, with a Shrike-armed A-4 tucked in so close that DRV radar operators would discern only a single blip. When the Fan Song went to high PRF (pulse repetition frequency), the EA-3B would pass heading information to the "Scooter" to shoot. In at least one case, a Fan Song then went abruptly off air, its crew either killed or intimidated.

BELOW WILD WEASEL'S FIRST KILL

On December 22, 1965, pilot Captain Al Lamb and EWO Capt Jack Donovan of the 6234th TFW (Wild Weasel Detachment) led the first successful Wild Weasel hunter-killer mission to destroy a SA-2 site. Flying F-100F Super Sabre SN 58-1226, they led Spruce Flight – four 388th TFW F-105Ds piloted by flight lead Captain Don Langwell (Spruce 1), Van Heywood (Spruce 2), Bob Bush (Spruce 3), and Art Brattkus (Spruce 4). The mission took off from Korat RTAFB at 0900 local time, to support a *Rolling Thunder* strike on Yen Bai, and air-refueled over Laos before proceeding NNE and turning E after crossing into the DRV. The flight descended from 16,000ft to 300ft. The F-100 led, with the four F-105s, flying as two pairs, weaving behind so as not to overrun the slower F-100F. The pairs were separated from each other by 2,000 to 4,000ft, trailing the F-100F by about the same distance.

Donovan detected the characteristic Fan Song signal 100 miles away from the site, and as the F-100F got closer, the signal grew in strength. The flight descended over the DRV down to 300ft AGL, the F-100F and F-105Ds using terrain masking to shield themselves, popping up from 300 to 1,300ft to get direction-finding cuts, and using those updates to edge closer. In the last portion of the flight, the Vector radar warning scope was showing strong strobes reaching 2½ rings, indicating the Fan Song was at high pulse repetition frequency (PRF) and tracking the flight. Then, in the last seconds, it hit 3 rings, and the strobes started to curl at their ends, indicating extremely close proximity. Lamb and Donovan climbed to 2,500ft, rolled inverted, and Lamb spotted the Fan Song fire control van camouflaged to look like a village hut, as well as "three long, white missiles under a thatched hut." He rolled upright and fired two pods of 2.75in rockets which landed short, but then strafed as well with the F-100F's 20mm cannon, exploding one missile. The yellow-orange blast marked the site for the F-105Ds which launched their own attacks with 2.75in rockets and strafing, destroying it utterly.

The flight detected a second Fan Song signal, but, being out of weapons, turned for Korat, still at low altitude. They climbed to 5,000ft over western NVN, then back to 16,000ft over Laos before again tanking prior to the return back to Korat. After landing, a historic signal was sent to the Pentagon: "Wild Weasel sighted SAM site—Destroyed same."

The Navy's use of tactical radar-hunters attracted Air Force interest and led to Lieutenant Commander Trent R. "Dick" Powers, operations officer of VA-164 off *Oriskany* volunteering to path-find for Thud SAM-hunters out of Takhli. On October 31, amid foul weather, he led eight F-105Ds (four apiece from the 334th and 562nd TFSs) against SAM sites near Doi Ngo in the Ha Bac area. Powers' A-4E had an ECM package that helped shield the flight from numerous SAMs launched against it, and a radar homing receiver to find the Fan Song. He located one site and bombed it from 50ft with 500lb Mk 82 drag-retarded bombs he had brought from the *O* boat; the eight Thuds destroyed two others by popping up to 7,500ft and dive-bombing with 750lb M-117s. While the Thuds avoided loss, Powers was shot down and killed directly over the site by withering light flak, his courage so impressing the Thud pilots that they recommended him for the Air Force Cross (he received the Navy Cross instead).

These early strikes illustrated for Americans the need for better technology, tactics, techniques, and procedures, but also showed that the SAM sites were far from invulnerable, and, for the Vietnamese, that their SAM crews – many hastily drawn from technical school and shop, and thus not "hardened" military cadres – could be cowed and intimidated. A Bullpup attack on a SAM site at Yen Vuong, north-northeast of Kép, took the 63rd Battalion out of service, while an attack against the 65th Battalion, caught while assembling SA-2s at Mieu Mon, southwest of Hanoi, killed the battalion commander and other senior staff. A series of TF-77 attacks on the 62nd Battalion at Dong Giao, midway between Hanoi and Haiphong, rendered it combat ineffective, triggered dissatisfaction and loss of confidence among troops of the screening 212th and 250th AA regiments, and resulted in official recriminations and mandatory unit self-examination.

In August 1965, coincidental with Iron Hand, the Air Force launched Wild Weasel I, modifying four two-place North American F-100Fs with radar warning receivers, signal strength and direction finders, and a SAM launch warning indicator to act as SAM-locators for killer F-105 strike flights. A two-man crew – pilot and electronic warfare officer (EWO) – would fly the mission. After tests against a Fan Song simulator at Eglin Air Force Base, Florida, they departed for Korat RTAFB in late November 1965, being designated the 6234th TFW Wild Weasel Det. The F-100Fs entered combat on December 19, suffering their first loss (to conventional AAA near Kép) the next day with the pilot taken captive and the EWO killed, apparently in a shoot-out while courageously resisting PAVN soldiers. Just days later, on December 22, Captains Allen T. Lamb and John E. Donovan gained a measure of revenge, stalking Fan Song emissions south of Yen Bai, locating the site, and marking it for accompanying 388th TFW Thuds to destroy, Wild Weasel's first victory.

By early 1966, however, the F-100F had revealed that it could not keep up with the faster Thuds, which had to follow a weaving flight path behind the arrowing "Hun" as it made its way to a target. Unsurprisingly, the two-place Thud – technically Wild Weasel III (Wild Weasel II, an interim modified F-105, was canceled in development) – replaced the two-place F-100F. Five F-105F Wild Weasels arrived at Korat RTAFB in May, flying their first missions with the 388th TFW in June. Takhli received six that month, putting them over the North with the 355th TFW in early July. The Air Force converted a further 52 F-105Fs, later upgrading surviving Weasels as F-105Gs.

Wild Weasel crews took high casualties, for, unlike strike aircraft passing through a target area, the Weasels lingered as long as a half-hour or more deep in the midst of heavy defenses, which, by late summer 1966, consisted both of conventional AAA and SAMs, and also MiGs. DRV SA-2 teams typically fired salvos of three missiles against a targeted airplane, leading to huge SA-2 consumption rates that taxed Soviet logistical support, particularly given disruptions caused by the Sino-Soviet rivalry and internal troubles within the PRC caused by Mao's "Cultural Revolution," but which greatly endangered SAM-hunters as well. Until crews gained combat expertise, initial casualties were high: 45 days after Takhli received its first six Weasel Thuds, all had been lost, with nine of their sixteen crewmen dead, wounded, or captured (another one quit). "I believe everybody was pretty fatalistic, but not overly concerned," Takhli Weasel EWO Kevin "Mike" Gilroy recalled; "Getting shot down, being taken prisoner, or getting killed was not something you sat around and talked about." Overall, more than 17 percent – 11 of 63 – of all F-105F Wild Weasel conversions were lost to enemy fire.

The courage of SAM-hunters bred a special respect. Two 355th TFW Wild Weasels – Captain Merlyn Dethlefsen and Major Leo Thorsness – received the Medal of Honor, America's highest award for valor, for missions on, respectively, March 10, 1967 and April 19, 1967. So, too, did Lieutenant Commander Michael Estocin, a Navy A-4 SAM-killer from *Ticonderoga's* VA-192, his sadly posthumously, for two counter-SAM missions he flew on April 20 and 26, 1967, the latter at the cost of his life. Thorsness did not receive his Medal of Honor until 1973: he was shot down by an unseen MiG-21 and, together with his EWO, taken prisoner on April 30, 1967 on his 93rd mission "Up North," enduring an imprisonment so brutal that he entitled a memoir *Surviving Hell*. A number of SAM-killers – including Lieutenant Colonel James McInerney, Captains Kevin "Mike" Gilroy, Harold Johnson, Fred Shannon, and the previously mentioned Lieutenant Commander Dick Powers – received an Air Force or Navy Cross.

SA-2s FIRED VERSUS AIRCRAFT LOST, 1965–68[1]				
Year	Estimated DRV SA-2 Sites[2]	Total SA-2s Known Fired[3]	Total Aircraft Lost	SA-2s Fired per Aircraft Lost
1965	64	194	11	17.64 : 1
1966	137	1,096	31	35.35 : 1
1967	229	3,202	62[4]	51.65 : 1
1968[5]	189	526	8	65.75 : 1

Notes
1 From Momyer, Air Power in Three Wars, p. 136; and Davies, F-105 Wild Weasel vs. SA-2 Guideline, pp. 71–75.
2 From USAF, Southeast Asia Review 1961–1973, MS (C6)m May 6, 1974, p. 32. Total at end of CY; not all are necessarily operational at the same time.
3 Total US-confirmed SA-2 launches is 4,814; total aircrew claimed launches (including multiple sightings of the same launch/missile) ≈9,000; total DRV acknowledged SA-2 launches is 5,800.
4 Davies, F-105 Wild Weasel vs. SA-2 Guideline, pp. 71, 73.
5 For January–March only, data from CHECO, Rolling Thunder Jan 1967–Nov 1968.

Over time, as shown in the table above, the combination of jamming, direct attack, and ALQ-71 and ALQ-87 barrage-jamming electronic self-protection pods (added in early 1967 to ingressing Thuds and F-4s) markedly reduced the efficiency of the SA-2, as measured by the rising number of SA-2s needed to down a *Rolling Thunder* attacker, which went from a highly lethal 17.64 in 1965 to a still dangerous but tolerable 65.75 in 1968. In 1967, the peak year of *Rolling Thunder*, DRV active SAM sites exploited 1,104 firing opportunities, during which they launched 3,202 SA-2s, destroying 62 airplanes.

This statistic does not, of course, indicate one of the SA-2's most dangerous side-effects, namely forcing strike aircraft to dive to low altitude to frustrate the SA-2's terminal guidance, thereby placing themselves deep within the threat envelope of conventional antiaircraft guns, particularly 57mm rapid-firing cannon. "Even though the SAMs didn't get many direct kills," Momyer wrote after the war, "they contributed importantly to the overall defense system by forcing our operations down to an altitude at which another part of the system was more effective." (The same occurred in 1973, when SA-6s forced Israeli aircraft down into range of SA-7 shoulder-fired SAMs and the deadly ZSU-23-4 gun carriage.) Certainly, for example, of the over 80 percent F-105 losses attributable to conventional AAA, many stemmed from Thuds driven to lower altitude while evading SA-2s already in

BELOW F-105 ECM FORMATIONS

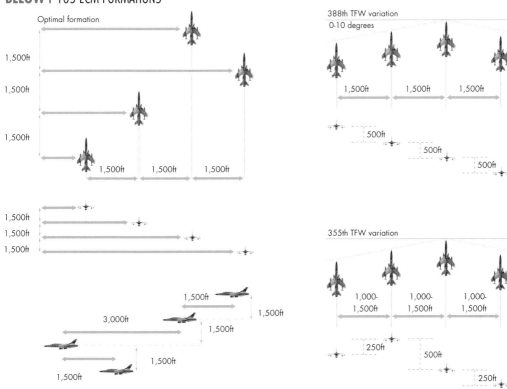

the air. The addition of jamming pods, while requiring rigorous formation flying for mutual support, enabled ingressing aircraft like the Thud to go back up to medium altitudes, above most conventional AAA.

Finally, among the many missed opportunities *Rolling Thunder* presented for proper air power application, there was the case of 132 SA-2 loaded canisters spotted in early May 1966 by a SAC reconnaissance drone at a barracks at Gia Thuong, near Gia Lam airport. The cache was large enough to outfit 11 SA-2 battalions. Not surprisingly, Admiral Grant Sharp pressed for an immediate attack, noting it would give Hanoi's air defenders "a severe blow." But this time it was the JCS, not McNamara or his minions, who said no. So it went untouched, and one wonders whose life, or at least freedom, was possibly forfeited by that fateful decision.

One of the beneficial byproducts of the Iron Hand and Wild Weasel effort was the intimidation of SAM operators. Firing statistics indicate that SAM crews became notably far less willing to shoot, lest they expose themselves to counterattacks that typically involved exploding Shrikes, cluster munitions, blasts of 2.75in rockets, M-117 bombs, and even the SAMs themselves with their large warheads and toxic, corrosive propellants. The presence of Shrike anti-radar missile shooters resulted in lower SAM firing rates even when clear opportunities presented themselves. Over the last year of *Rolling Thunder*, Shrike shooters fired 1,146 Shrikes, claiming 370 Fan Songs destroyed or damaged: during that same period, SAM teams fired on average only once for every three firing opportunities. Even SAM battalion commanders were intimidated, one refusing to launch, claiming that jamming prevented his seeing any target, even though an American airplane on his scope was plainly visible to a visiting PAVN senior officer!

BELOW DRV COMMAND POST-REORGANIZATION

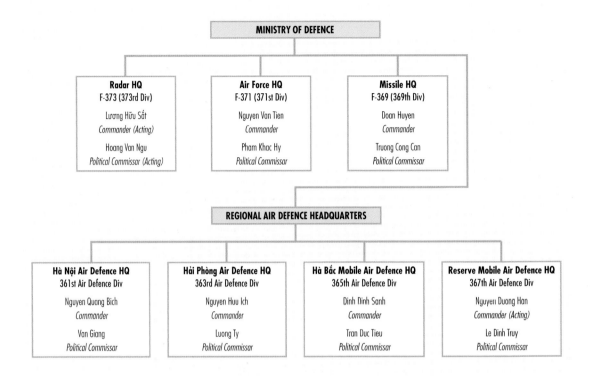

The Weasel/Iron Hand threat resulted in an astonishing example of Marxist–Leninist favoritism: the PAVN chose to value the well-being of Soviet PVO-Strany personnel over the People's Liberation Army (PLA) AA troops! As air power historian Xiaoming Zhang noted, "Hanoi arranged for Soviet surface-to-air missile units to redeploy to avoid US Wild Weasel and Iron Hand anti-SAM attacks, but moved Chinese antiaircraft units into the positions previously occupied by the Soviets. The Chinese, therefore, were disproportionately targeted by the often-deadly counter-SAM missile, bomb, and strafing attacks." This and other perceived Vietnamese ingratitude towards the PRC and its "volunteers" then serving in the DRV at risk to their lives undid the fulsome "Your business is my business and my business is your business" pledge that Mao had made to PAVN General Van Tien Dung in June 1964. (Relations between the Hanoi and Beijing regimes steadily declined, eventually resulting in Deng Xiaoping launching a "show more respect" invasion of Vietnam by the People's Liberation Army in 1979.)

From April 1966 through March 1967, the ADF-VPAF command staff evinced steadily growing concern over American jamming; the Wild Weasels; and the inability of radar, AA, and SAM units to detect low-flying aircraft, defeat hard-maneuvering targets, overcome heavy jamming, and defeat the AGM-45 Shrike. The failure of air defenders to adequately confront raids around Hanoi in mid-March 1967 – particularly the high-speed of the F-105s – revealed inadequate coordination among AAA, SAMs, and MiGs, bad placement of conventional AAA in relation to target locations, and inefficient organizational structure, the latter leading to a major reorganization of regional air defense commands on March 24, 1967, the new structure being shown in the table above. Even so, however, American airmen still confounded it, setting standards for electronic combat that led to the more effective weapons, tactics, techniques, and procedures (including "stealth") that proved so crucial in *Desert Storm*.

Air interdiction

On April 1, 1965, *Rolling Thunder*'s interdiction effort against North Vietnam's rail and highway system began, and, as well, the US Air Force executed the first B-52 Arc Light bombing mission over the South. On April 3, the Navy and Air Force set out to drop two of the DRV's bridges. That day, TF-77 launched 62 strike aircraft – 35 A-4s, 18 F-8s, 5 F-4s, and 4 A-1s – against the Dong Phong Thong railway and highway bridge near Thanh Hoa. Dropping a total of 184 bombs and firing 72 2.75in Folding Fin Aerial Rockets (FFAR), the A-4/F-8 strikers dropped the bridge's center span at the price of an A-4 lost to flak. That same day, following a delay occasioned by lack of tanker support coupled with marginal weather, the Air Force launched *Rolling Thunder IX-Alpha*, a package of 46 F-105Ds, capped by 21 F-100Ds, with ten KC-135 tankers for support and two RF-101 recce aircraft striking the nearby Ham Rong ("Dragon's Jaw") bridge. Spanning the Song Ma (Ma river) northeast of Thanh Hoa, this 540ft steel-and-concrete heavily abutted behemoth carried two roads and a railroad track, having been completed with Chinese technical assistance just a year earlier, in 1964. Known to air planners and airmen as simply the "Thanh Hoa bridge," JCS Target 14, it soon became emblematic of the frustrations of *Rolling Thunder* interdiction attacks in the pre-precision weapon era, and a notorious flak trap for attacking aircraft. Even then it was protected by two 57mm batteries, two 37mm batteries, a battery of heavy machine guns, and antiaircraft guns on DRV naval vessels moored in the Song Ma river, as well as a GCI-controlled CAP of MiG-17 fighters.

Sixteen of the Thuds carried two Martin AGM-12A Bullpup air-to-surface missiles, and the rest carried eight M-117 750lb general purpose bombs, six on a centerline triple ejector rack (TER) and two on each outer wing pylon, some having as well 2.75in FFAR pods. The bridge suffered little damage, at the cost of an F-100D and its pilot lost. Early Bullpups, while accurate, had only a 250lb warhead and thus did little but scratch the massive bridge (some even bounced off before detonating) while the need to be steered into a target exposed their launch pilots to great risk. (Cool-headed North Vietnamese gunners shot back through the Bullpup's missile exhaust, knowing they had a good chance of hitting the trailing attacker that fired it.)

The Thuds flew a restrike on the Dragon's Jaw late the next morning, dropping 384 M-117s and firing 32 AGM-12s, scoring several hits that damaged a section of the bridge, at the cost of an F-105D shot down by flak. "Clearly, this was an indication not only of the difficulties that would be encountered in hitting such targets, but also of mounting an interdiction effort against well-defended North Vietnamese lines of communications," an Air Force interdiction study concluded, adding: "For the next few weeks, message traffic

Dive-bombing the Phuong Dinh Bridge

On September 10, 1967, Douglas A-4E Skyhawks from *Oriskany*'s VA-163 and VA-164 attacked the Phuong Dinh Railroad Bridge Bypass, a target with multiple bypasses and antiaircraft sites, exemplifying why bridge attacks in the pre-precision era were both frustrating and dangerous.

This scene depicts a moment toward the end of the attack, which included both bridge bombers and flak suppressors. The flak-suppressing A-4s struck from low level while the bridge bombers dived from higher altitude.

The dive-bomber pulling directly off target at top left has completed its bomb run, releasing its bombs at about 6,500ft and levelling out no lower than 4,500ft to avoid light flak. The bombers would dive initially at 50–60 degrees to get to their drop altitude quickly and prevent heavy flak (typically 85mm) from targeting them, then transition to a descending, weaving, jinking approach at about a 30–35-degree angle, steadying only briefly (3–4 seconds maximum) before dropping their bombs at about 6,500ft, with a 4–5g pull-out, then a hard left break and a weaving and jinking egress to the east toward the Gulf of Tonkin.

Reconnaissance crews, flying aircraft such as this Vought RF-8A Crusader (BuNo 146897) of the *Oriskany* (CVA-34) VFP-63 photo detachment shown over South Vietnam in July 1966, furnished the raw imagery which analysts turned into the actionable intelligence that strike planners used to develop target lists. But getting such imagery came at great risk; for example, 15 recce Crusaders were lost to enemy fire in SEA. (NHHC)

between the JCS, CINCPAC, CINCPACAF, Thirteenth AF, and 2nd AD concerned possible tactics and ordnance improvements which might tumble the stubborn span... Three years later the bridge still stood." (It eventually fell for good under the punishing blows of 24 laser-guided bombs assisted by 48 conventional ones on May 13, 1972, during Operation *Linebacker*.)

1966–67

New targets: POL, bridges, and power plants

Over 1965, *Rolling Thunder* resembled in some respects a "working up" period for the far more intense air war that followed in 1966 – following a 37-day bombing halt from December 24, 1965 to January 31, 1966 during which the DRV used the time to rebuild and accelerate its infiltration – and, especially, 1967. Over this time, as discussed previously, commanders in the field thrashed out working arrangements among their forces, while in Washington, the JCS grappled with the Johnson administration's innate hesitancy to hit the targets that really might have influenced the war in the South, namely the docks and logistical centers, and petroleum distribution and storage well inside the North, around Hanoi and Haiphong. Subsequently, of course, the whole problem of confronting the SA-2 acted as its own distraction from the kind of limited straight-forward "road recce"-based campaign that McNamara and others had thought they could prosecute.

Indeed, by the time of the 1965 Honolulu conference, McNamara was criticizing the road recce effort, the beginning of his own growing disillusionment with *Rolling Thunder*. At another Honolulu conference in January 1966, PACOM's Sharp, supported by the JCS, advocated for a more aggressive and broader air and naval war; the next month, McNamara rejected this, stressing that American objectives were "very, very limited," and (once again concerned lest he ruffle the Beijing and Hanoi regimes) certainly not "to destroy or to overthrow the Communist government of China or the Communist government of Vietnam." In October 1966, in a memo sent to Johnson, he noted glumly that "Enemy morale has not broken," and that "Pacification is a bad disappointment," adding, "Nor has the *Rolling Thunder* program of bombing the North either significantly affected infiltration or cracked the morale of Hanoi."

He then proposed a physical barrier running across the neck of South Vietnam and Laos, mixing sensors, barriers, and mobile forces: it was a long way and a far sight removed from his initial concept of using "armed reconnaissance" sorties to sever the Ho Chi Minh Trail, and reflected a recommendation of the Jasons, an elite scientific advisory panel. He proposed reducing *Rolling Thunder* down to a "stabilized" bombing program – in short, a steady level of violence, attrition, and human loss on both sides – to "remove the prospect of ever-escalating bombing as a factor complicating our political posture and distracting from the main job of pacification in South Vietnam." The memo triggered immediate protest from the Joint Chiefs, and subsequent resistance at the Manila conference on the war held later that month, from William Westmoreland. When, in early July 1967 on the eve of a Saigon conference, McNamara proposed halting bombing above the 20th Parallel as an enticement for the North Vietnamese to enter peace negotiations, only strenuous arguments by Wheeler, the JCS, Sharp, Momyer, and Admiral John Hyland (commander of the Seventh Fleet) convinced him not to do so.

By the spring of 1967, McNamara was actively opposed to further air action, effectively strangling the infant of his own conception. He continued to resist attacking the North's ports, indeed any "additional military targets north of 20°," recommending instead that "all of the sorties allocated to the *Rolling Thunder* program be concentrated on lines of communications" between the 17th and 20th Parallels. Westmoreland and Earle Wheeler vigorously opposed McNamara's increasing determination to curtail air power, and the JCS concurred with them, still advocating for an expanded air campaign including mining all coastal waters and harbors.

The table below gives a breakdown of *Rolling Thunder* attack sorties by year and service, including the Strategic Air Command's growing role in furnishing Arc Light B-52 missions over the North in an effort to interdict the trail. Over 1965, the US Navy flew almost 20 percent more attack sorties over the North (13,783) than the US Air Force (11,599). While, admittedly, the Air Force had much larger requirements supporting the very different air war over South Vietnam (its airmen flew 36,299 attack sorties over the South that year compared to the Navy's 18,825 and the Marine Corps' 10,798), the Navy's air war over North Vietnam was remarkable for its steadfastness and persistence from *Rolling Thunder*'s earliest days to its end, and on through the final end to the Vietnam air war in 1973. As the F-105 carried the great burden of Air Force strikes, so the A-4 did for the Navy, and also at a stiff cost: 196 lost in combat.

A flight of 355th TFW Republic F-105D Thunderchiefs, affectionately known as "Thuds," air-refueling from a Boeing KC-135 Stratotanker before ingressing into "Pack Six" during 1966. The F-105D (SN 62-4228) in the foreground is *Alice's Joy*, flown by the 355th TFW's charismatic vice commander Colonel Jacksel "Jack" Broughton. (NARA)

ROLLING THUNDER STRIKE SORTIES BY SERVICE, 1965–68[1]						
	USAF	USN	USMC	Total Joint Service Strike[2]	SAC Arc Light	Year Total
1965	11,599	13,783	26	25,408	0	25,408
1966	44,482	32,954	3,695	81,131	223	81,354
1967	54,316	42,587	8,672	105,575	1,364	106,939
1968[3]	41,057	40,848	10,326	92,231	686	92,917
Grand totals	151,454	130,172	22,719	304,345	2,273	306,618
Percentage	49.40%	42.45	7.41%	99.26%	00.74%	100.00%

Notes

1 From Van Staaveren, Toward a Bombing Halt, OAFH 1970, Table 3, p. 70.

2 Not including SAC B-52 Arc Light sorties.

3 January–March only.

For example, at the end of the 1965 the Navy deployed two of its three nuclear-powered surface ships – the carrier *Enterprise* (CVAN-65, then the world's largest warship), and the frigate *Bainbridge* (DLGN-25) – to Tonkin Gulf. After blooding its air wing with strikes against the Viet Cong, *Enterprise* set vigorously to work, setting a then-record for the most carrier-launched combat sorties in a single day (165), and teaming with the air wings off *Kitty Hawk* and *Ticonderoga* to launch the first 100-plane Alpha strike employed against a DRV industrial target, the Uong Bi thermal power plant near Haiphong.

This particular target was struck numerous times by TF-77, who bombed it as quickly as DRV workers rebuilt it, most notably on the night of April 18, 1966, when two A-6A Intruders of *Kitty Hawk's* VA-85 catapulted off the ship deep into the night, flew at 500ft most of the way to the target, popped up to accurately drop 13 Mk 83 1,000lb bombs from a safe altitude, and retired safely as the night sky behind them erupted in explosions and too-late flak.

The air war over North Vietnam changed significantly in the spring of 1966 as the Johnson administration was forced to confront the inadequacies of its gradualist interdiction campaign. That February, in successive memos, the Joint Chiefs again had urged bombing the DRV's POL stocks and infrastructure. This time McNamara – likely to their surprise

The Haiphong cement plant complex after having been struck by *Kitty Hawk's* CVW-11 on April 27, 1967. (NHHC)

The Thai Nguyen complex during the May 10, 1967 raid by Korat and Takhli Thuds. (NMUSAF)

– agreed to attack seven of nine targets they proposed. In early May, Walt Rostow (who had replaced McGeorge Bundy as National Security Advisor the previous month) went further, recommending a POL campaign like that pursued with great success against Nazi Germany in 1944–45. Out of this came *Rolling Thunder 50*, a concept for comprehensive joint service attacks against the seven selected POL storage targets (at Bac Giang, Do Son, Duong Nham, Haiphong, Hanoi, Nguyen Ke, and Phuc Yen), an early warning radar site at Kép, the Viet Trì railroad–highway bridge, and Haiphong's thermal power plant and cement plant. Strike planners at Seventh Air Force (as 2nd Air Division became, on April 1, 1966) and on TF-77's carriers set to work, though, for various reasons, the first strikes did not take place until June 29, 1966.

Air Force and Navy strikes over the spring and summer of 1967 on the Hanoi cement plant, power plants at Uong Bi, Hanoi, and at the Thai Nguyen industrial complex, and against POL targets were temporarily productive, though not lastingly so. Power targets, seemingly battered into ruin, quickly came back on line. In the case of POL, the North Vietnamese countered by switching from centralized storage to dispersed storage, evident from photographs of Soviet supply ships which, having once simply pumped their cargo ashore, now delivered it in barrels, beginning in August 1966. Absent strikes on Haiphong's docks, and attacks on other, smaller storage facilities, the POL campaign could achieve no more, and so gradually withered, though strikes continued into the fall against all seven of the selected storage targets, and, as well, against oil barges, tank cars, and receiving terminals.

First strike on Hanoi's oil plants

On June 29, 1966, the Navy and Air Force took on Hanoi's POL infrastructure. *Ranger* and *Constellation's* air wings launched Alpha strikes against the Haiphong and Do Son POL complexes, which erupted in towering fireballs, while, to the west, the 355th TFW and 388th TFW launched two back-to-back strikes on the outskirts of Hanoi that burned a fifth of the DRV's fuel reserves, with billowing eruptions and thick black smoke visible from across the North Vietnamese capital. It was, wrote strike leader Major James H. Kasler (operations officer of the 354th TFS), "an unbelievable sight. As I climbed back to about 5,000 feet I could see flames leaping out of the smoke thousands of feet above me." Afterwards, at the yearly Honolulu conference where American and South Vietnamese political and military leaders met to discuss the war and its strategy, Lyndon Johnson announced that POL was now *Rolling Thunder's* top targeting priority.

QUI VINH RR BR
9 APRIL 1965

DESTROYED SPAN

As part of *Rolling Thunder X*, 48 F-105s struck the Qui Vinh, Khe Kiem, and Phuong Can bridges on April 9, 1965, dropping all three without loss. Here is a post-strike photograph showing the Qui Vinh bridge, shot by an Air Force McDonnell RF-101 Voodoo reconnaissance aircraft. (USIA via NHHC)

By the end of April 1965, American and South Vietnamese airmen had destroyed or damaged 22 bridges on Routes 1 (Bernard Fall's famed "Street Without Joy"), 7, 8, and 12, and on some connecting roads as well. But bridge strikes weren't as productive as hoped. In the pre-precision laser-guided or GPS-cued bomb era, few bombs actually hit, those that did were usually too small to do much damage, and guided glide bombs like Walleye or missiles like Bullpup, while having the accuracy, had other limitations that worked against them. North Vietnamese militias and repair crews worked around bridge cuts by building simple bypasses (eventually 292 temporary wooden bypasses were built, and 500 bypasses of other types such as pontoon bridges, causeways, ferry slips, and fords). Work crews generally restored the original bridges quickly, in part because there were nearly 100,000 full-time civil engineering workers (20,000 of which were Chinese) working on the problem, assisted by almost 200,000 part-time workers. Overall, CIA analysts estimated that repairing damage to the DRV's bridges consumed over $30 million (approximately $210 million in 2017) by the end of *Rolling Thunder*. In June 1966, a CIA analysis sent to Walt Rostow concluded that despite a year of air attacks on the DRV's transportation infrastructure, "the resultant damage was relatively light, in good measure reflecting the restricted nature of the air campaign."

In short, in the pre-precision era, and as in Korea previously, the anti-bridge campaign in *Rolling Thunder* stood little chance of permanent success. Arguably, the transportation campaign's greatest contribution was tying down manpower, both for air defense and for road and bridge repair. In addition to the nearly 300,000 workers focused on bridge repair, 70,000 troops who could have been fighting were instead tied up on air defense duty.

As calculated by CIA economists, every dollar's worth of damage to North Vietnam cost American taxpayers $8.70 ($66.00 in 2017). But this did not include aircraft losses: PACOM averaged over $53 million (approximately $388 million in 2017) in lost aircraft *per month*, many shot down revisiting much-hit targets, or targets of little intrinsic value. Harbor mining, urged by PACOM's Sharp and others, constituted a potentially tremendously cost-effective means of exerting leverage against Hanoi, but, aside from some mining of rivers, was not pursued. Instead, strikers persisted in road and bridge cuts, losing numerous aircraft to deployed AAA and SAM sites, and facing risk from the occasional MiG foray.

Still, there were success stories: on August 11, 1967, Thud pilots led by Colonel Robert White, formerly the Air Force's chief X-15 pilot (and first pilot to fly a winged aircraft at Mach 4, 5, and 6), dropped the center span of the Paul Doumer railroad and highway bridge, a key transportation target, knocking down other spans on subsequent raids.

The Doumer raid came at a time when McNamara and *Rolling Thunder* were facing bitter Congressional criticism from members of the President's own party, including Senator Stuart Symington, a former Secretary of the Air Force who was so insistent about bombing Phuc Yen that JCS Chairman Wheeler told Lyndon Johnson the Missouri Democrat was "like a broken record." In August, Johnson, increasingly desperate and looking towards the 1968 Presidential election, proposed ending *Rolling Thunder* if Hanoi would stop infiltrating troops and supplies into the South. Realizing he had simply confirmed that their "talk–fight" strategy was working, the DRV leadership refused his offer. Then Senator John Stennis (D-Miss) oversaw hearings of the Senate Preparedness Investigating Subcommittee of the Committee on Armed Services that sharply criticized the conduct of the war, with numerous senior witnesses – including Admiral U. S. Grant Sharp – attacking its underlying strategy and intent and, both directly and indirectly, its chief architect, Robert McNamara.

The Stennis hearings furnished the most incendiary military theater since the fiery roles and missions debate of the late 1940s and the Army–McCarthy hearings of the early 1950s. When they were over, McNamara was done as well, and by extension, his concept of *Rolling Thunder*. Under questioning, he had fought back vigorously, still advancing the merits of below-the-20th-Parallel gradualism, but the old number-based magic he had worked so long was gone. "He was always forceful, opinionated, and unwilling to concede a single point to his inquisitors," Secretary of Defense historian Edward Drea wrote, "But three years of Vietnam [had] destroyed his credibility, discredited his policies, and shattered his aura of infallibility."

The Stennis hearings strengthened the hand of the Joint Chiefs. Afterwards, Wheeler, as Chairman of the JCS, joined the Tuesday targeting luncheons as a regular, not occasional participant. High on the JCS's priorities was attacking Phuc Yen. Still, McNamara, in a meeting with Johnson, Rusk, and Generals McConnell and H. K. Johnson, demurred, as usual worrying over Chinese intervention. But then, on October 23, facing DRV intransigence and antiwar protests in the States, Lyndon Johnson met with his national security team and ordered Phuc Yen struck: "Now we have gotten rid of all the excuses," he said, "Let's go with it."

It is possible that Johnson was reacting to more than North Vietnamese intransigence over negotiations. As confirmed by his White House diary, on October 2, he had a private 35-minute meeting with Colonel Robin Olds, who had led Operation *Bolo*, and who then held the record – four – for most VPAF MiGs shot down. Olds was passing through Washington, en route to his next assignment as Commandant of Cadets at the Air Force Academy. It was supposed to be a public relations grip-and-grin, but when Johnson asked Olds about the war, the fighter pilot went characteristically off-script.

"The way to end this war is just to end the damned thing!" he exclaimed, condemning McNamara-style gradualism and detailing the kinds of targets that needed to be attacked. "Startled," Johnson listened, thanked him, and asked him to meet with National Security Advisor Walt Rostow the next day. When he did, Rostow – "deeply concerned that anything more than we were already doing would broaden the conflict beyond control,"

Task Force 77 Alpha Strike into Route Pack VIB

1967

Kep

2

Kep

7

5

Kien An

HAIPHONG

Cat Bi

6

EVENTS

1. Alpha strike package from Carrier Air Wing 19 (CVW-19) aboard the USS *Ticonderoga* (CVA-14) approaches coast of North Vietnam, ingressing at 350kts at 20,000ft.

2. Flight of four MiG-17 Fresco-Cs of the VPAF's 923rd Regiment "Yen The" takes off from Kep. On ground, SAM sites ready for first launches based on tracking information from their Fan Song fire-control radars.

3. Alpha strike leader begins descent to roll-in altitude, jinking and weaving to confound gunners during descent. Alerted by radar warning receivers, Iron Hand sections begun hunting SAM radars, firing on four of them with Shrikes. TARCAP remains high and moves to outside to block MiGs from attacking strike forces.

4. Kep GCI orders MiG-17 flight, now at 10,000ft, to turn south and climb, positioning it to engage strike by attacking from astern – but the MiG attacks are frustrated by the F-8 TARCAP.

5. VA-192 A-4F and VF-194 F-8E strike package reaches 14,000ft roll-in point amid increasingly heavy conventional antiaircraft fire. The package rolls in on Kien An Airbase and drops its bombs at 4,500ft altitude, clearing the target within two minutes, and then climbs back to egress altitude. The Iron Hand and F-8 flak suppressors continue attacking SAM and AAA sites, and F-8 TARCAP frustrates the MiG-17s, which repeatedly attempt to engage strike force.

6. The strike package and escorts disengage, jinking, weaving and climbing to altitude. Iron Hand sections and TARCAP cover their egress and disengage last.

7. GCI vectors MiGs, now at 8,500ft, to return to Kep. They dodge through their own 85mm and 100mm antiaircraft fire.

8. Alpha strike is now all "feet wet" over the Gulf of Tonkin. USS Ticonderoga launches a single RF-8G (VFP-63 Det 14) plus a single F-8E (VF-191) escort to undertake post-strike low-level recce of target.

ALTITUDES
US

	8,000–20,000ft
	6,500–20,000ft
	6,000–20,000ft
	10,000–22,000ft

NV

	2,500–16,000ft

KEY

 VPAF Airfield

Mobile SA-2 SAM sites

GULF OF TONKIN

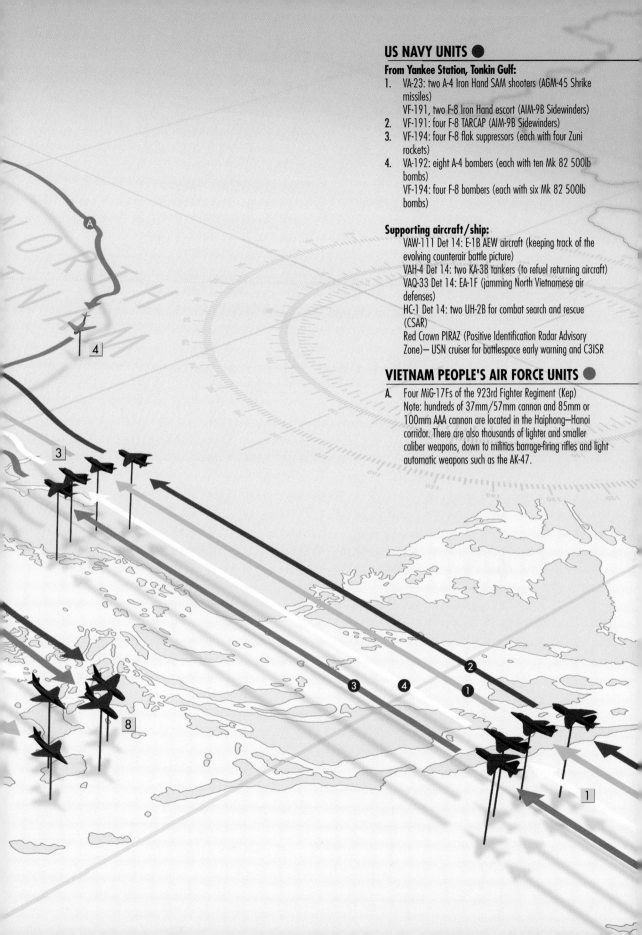

US NAVY UNITS ●

From Yankee Station, Tonkin Gulf:
1. VA-23: two A-4 Iron Hand SAM shooters (AGM-45 Shrike missiles)
   VF-191, two F-8 Iron Hand escort (AIM-9B Sidewinders)
2. VF-191: four F-8 TARCAP (AIM-9B Sidewinders)
3. VF-194: four F-8 flak suppressors (each with four Zuni rockets)
4. VA-192: eight A-4 bombers (each with ten Mk 82 500lb bombs)
   VF-194: four F-8 bombers (each with six Mk 82 500lb bombs)

Supporting aircraft/ship:
VAW-111 Det 14: E-1B AEW aircraft (keeping track of the evolving counterair battle picture)
VAH-4 Det 14: two KA-3B tankers (to refuel returning aircraft)
VAQ-33 Det 14: EA-1F (jamming North Vietnamese air defenses)
HC-1 Det 14: two UH-2B for combat search and rescue (CSAR)
Red Crown PIRAZ (Positive Identification Radar Advisory Zone)— USN cruiser for battlespace early warning and C3ISR

VIETNAM PEOPLE'S AIR FORCE UNITS ●

A. Four MiG-17Fs of the 923rd Fighter Regiment (Kep)
Note: hundreds of 37mm/57mm cannon and 85mm or 100mm AAA cannon are located in the Haiphong—Hanoi corridor. There are also thousands of lighter and smaller caliber weapons, down to militias barrage-firing rifles and light automatic weapons such as the AK-47.

Returning from an Alpha strike, Ling-Temco-Vought A-7A Corsair II (BuNo 153219) of VA-147, CVW-2, comes aboard *Ranger* (CVA-61), January 1968. (NHHC)

Olds recalled – raised the familiar specter of Chinese intervention. Olds left to take up his appointment, recalling afterwards "I only wanted to get the hell out of there." But that may not have been the end of it: it is quite possible that, on October 23, Johnson looked around at his advisors – collectively a colorless group of professional bureaucrats risking nothing – and, thinking of the charismatic fighter ace who had boldly risked his career in the Oval Office to set forth his views on the air war, opted for his airmen; if so, good for him – and good for Olds.

Targeting Phuc Yen met with jubilation in theater. At Takhli, 355th TFW pilots and maintainers had been readying for an afternoon strike into Route Pack VI when word came down of a target change: Phuc Yen. "This was the big strike we all had been waiting for," one pilot recalled, "and no one wanted to miss it." Immediately pounded by sequential strikes on October 24–25, Phuc Yen was thereafter struck repeatedly through the end of *Rolling Thunder*.

1968 and the end of *Rolling Thunder*

In January 1968, three thunderbolts hit: on January 21, the siege of Khe Sanh opened (resolute defense and massive air power would prevent a repetition of Dien Bien Phu); on January 23, the North Koreans seized the intelligence ship USS *Pueblo* (AGER-2, perhaps to draw off at least a portion of the Seventh Fleet from Tonkin Gulf and the South China Sea at a time when the DRV was preparing to spring the Tet offensive on an unsuspecting world); and then, on January 31 the immensely destructive Tet offensive began (in violation of a previously agreed truce). In response, air attacks concentrated on Pack I, strikes there soaring from 47 percent of all North Vietnam strikes in January 1968 to 72 percent in February. If nevertheless a military defeat for the PAVN and, especially, the Viet Cong, Tet constituted a strategic propaganda victory for the North, largely because of how the world's press and America's own news media reported it.

Though *Rolling Thunder* lingered until October 31, 1968, the end began with President Johnson's announcement, on March 31, 1968, of bombing restrictions, and also that America looked forward to negotiating a workable cease-fire agreement with the Hanoi regime, and that he would not seek a second term. On April 3, *Rolling Thunder* was restricted to Route Packs I, II, and III. In July, General Creighton Abrams replaced Westmoreland at MACV, and the next month the Seventh Air Force began "Vietnamization" of the air war. On November 1, Johnson announced a halt to all bombing of the North except for "protective reaction" in defense of reconnaissance missions, in effect returning Southeast Asia air power to the same rules of engagement that had initially existed in the early days of Laotian overflights. Critics suggested he had done so as a last-minute assist to Hubert Humphrey's lagging campaign for President, just four days away from the election.

If he had, it came too late: on November 5, 1968, for a variety of reasons including dissatisfaction over the course and direction of American participation in the Vietnam War, voters elected Richard M. Nixon as President. By then, Robert McNamara was ensconced as President of the World Bank; on November 28, 1967, he had tended his resignation as Secretary of Defense, effective at the end of February 1968. McGeorge Bundy was President of the Ford Foundation, having left the government in 1966. John McNaughton, who had ridiculed the SA-2 threat before Westmoreland and Moore, was dead: killed in July 1967 in a collision between a Piedmont Airlines 727 and a private Cessna 310 that also tragically took his wife and one son.

Debut of the F-111: March 25, 1968

In the fall of 1967, PACAF began deployment planning for its first General Dynamics F-111As, the initial Air Force version of the TFX (for "Tactical Fighter Experimental"), the most controversial of all of the McNamara era's joint-service "commonality" airplanes, intended as "cost effective" alternatives to aircraft procured via traditional acquisition processes. The F-4, OV-10, and A-7 programs demonstrated that, if properly conceived and executed, commonality could work, but with the TFX, McNamara had attempted the impossible – building a successful airplane by merging inherently contradictory requirements: a Navy requirement for a long-loiter fleet air defense fighter with a large and powerful radar and new long-range missiles; an Air Force requirement for a supersonic-dash nuclear and conventional strike aircraft; and the Kennedy administration's requirement that the resulting design also be capable of operating off austere airfields, reflecting its fixation on counterinsurgency (COIN). Key to meeting all these was a large variable-geometry wing that fully extended to generate the lift necessary to achieve long-range and long-loiter, but swept sharply back to reduce drag, permitting supersonic dash. In 1963, Congressional investigators found that the McNamara team had rejected the recommendations of service and NASA professionals when it selected General Dynamics over a more highly regarded Boeing design. Once in flight testing the TFX revealed serious performance and safety deficiencies, many requiring redesign. The F-111B carrier-based variant, greatly overweight and dangerously underpowered, never entered fleet service, forcing the Navy to develop a substitute, the Grumman F-14A Tomcat, which first flew over a dozen years after the F-4 had taken to the air.

For all the program's faults, the Air Force F-111A had great promise, combining attack avionics as good as the A-6's, a terrain-following radar (TFR) coupled to an autopilot, and low-level supersonic dash comparable to the speedy F-105. On March 17, 1968, St Patrick's Day, Combat Lancer – officially Det 1 of the 428th TFS, a six-aircraft operational test and evaluation force of the Air Force's new General Dynamics F-111A – landed at Takhli. The F-111A opened its combat career on March 25 with a night of strikes, beginning with a 500kt, 500ft solo attack that amply showcased the F-111A's abilities. Colonel Ivan Dethman and Captain Rick Matteis took off from Takhli in F-111A SN 66-0018, passed over Nakhon Phanom, and then descended to 500ft for a strike on the Vung Chua truck park and storage area on Hon Co Island. Dethman and Matteis dropped 12 M117 750lb bombs with drag-retarding fins before exiting over Tonkin Gulf.

Unfortunately, very quickly thereafter three were lost, two from mechanical failures and the third from an SA-2 (a fact considered so significant that then-Soviet defense minister Andrei Grechko personally briefed the shoot-down to Leonid Brezhnev), with just one crew being rescued. Like *Rolling Thunder* itself, the F-111A clearly needed further refinement. Though three additional F-111As arrived to make up for losses, Combat Lancer played little further role in Southeast Asia before returning to Nellis AFB in mid-November 1968. In 1972, the F-111A, now mature, returned to Vietnam, proving a deadly and highly effective night attacker during Operation *Linebacker*. Not quite two decades later, the superb F-111F, with greater power and the Pave Tack self-designating attack system, proved a stalwart of Operation *Desert Storm*.

AFTERMATH AND ANALYSIS

On 6 July 1966, 52 *Rolling Thunder* POWs were paraded through Hanoi before physically abusive crowds that regime propagandists had provoked into a frenzy. It drew immediate condemnation from global leaders including Pope Pius VI, UN Secretary General U Thant, and Prime Ministers Indira Gandhi and Harold Wilson. L-R (1st row) L–R: Richard Keirn and Kile Berg; (2nd row) L–R: Robert Schumaker and Carlyle "Smitty" Harris; (3rd row) L–R: Ronald Byrne and Lawrence Guarino; all survived to be released in 1973. (USAF)

Rolling Thunder ended for good on October 31. It left hundreds of airmen dead or injured, and hundreds more captive, languishing in barbaric conditions in prisons across the North, and routinely tortured, not only by their Vietnamese jailers, but also by a trio of Cubans whom the POWs dubbed Chico, Pancho, and Fidel (the latter seemingly their leader and, as well, the most notoriously brutal of the three). Of the 771 airmen who became POWs during the Vietnam War, 113 died in captivity, of whom 65 were tortured to death. "It was not information they wanted," Medal of Honor recipient Colonel Leo Thorsness wrote, "but propaganda: to get American military officers to condemn the war. They pursued this objective with single-minded brutality." Treatment of prisoners improved immediately after Ho Chi Minh died on September 2, 1969, convincing Colonel George "Bud" Day (another Medal of Honor awardee) and other POWs that "most of our pressure and mistreatment was his direct policy."

The Hanoi regime kept its POWs in filthy, vermin-ridden cells; denied them basic food, clothing, sanitation, and medical care; shackled and manacled them for weeks on end; repeatedly put them in solitary confinement that often lasted for months; deliberately humiliated them (including exposing them to abuse from onlookers and outsiders); berated them as "blackest criminals" beyond the protections of the Geneva Convention; threatened them with trials and the specter of endless incarceration; exploited them as bargaining chips in negotiations; denied them communication with relatives and the International Red Cross; and forced their unwilling participation in carefully staged propaganda events. Though often suffering from painful back injuries from the violent spinal kick imposed by older cartridge-type ejection seats, or with broken and dislocated bones and torn muscles and tissue from flailing arms and legs during transonic ejections at low and medium altitudes, POWs were subjected to savage beatings and outright torture by interrogators badgering them to confess to non-existent "war crimes." The DRV's torturers typically targeted their blows on a POW's existing injuries, thus ensuring they suffered permanent, career-ending disabilities, for medical treatment was extremely rare, and, if given, at best perfunctory, with little if any "follow-up."

The routine brutalization that POWs endured makes more impressive still the humanity and decency of those former POWs who, despite years of torture and deprivation, worked afterwards to build bonds between the people of the DRV and the United States, particularly naval aviator John McCain III (shot down October 26, 1967) and Air Force pilot Douglas "Pete" Peterson (shot down September 10, 1966), who became, in 1997, the first US Ambassador to the DRV, opening a new and welcome era in American–Vietnamese relations.

Rolling Thunder in numbers

US ATTACK SORTIES IN SOUTHEAST ASIA BY COUNTRY AND SERVICE, 1965–68[1]							
Country	Tactical Air Attacks by Military Service				SAC Arc Light	Total by Country	Percent by Country
	USAF	USN	USMC	Total			
South Vietnam	358,395	46,305	160,986	565,686	29,016	594,702	54.80
Service Attack Percentage	63.35	08.19	28.46	100.00			
North Vietnam	151,454	130,172	22,719	304,345	2,273	306,618	28.26
Service Attack Percentage	49.76	42.77	7.47	100.00			
Laos	132,305	31,890	13,856	178,051	5,761	183,812	16.94
Service Attack Percentage	74.31	17.91	7.78	100.00			
SEA Totals	642,154	208,367	197,561	1,048,082	37,050	1,085,132	100.00
Service Attack Percentage	61.27	19.88	18.85	100.00			

Notes
1 Computed from data in Van Staaveren, Toward a Bombing Halt, OAFH 1970, Table 3, p. 70. I have corrected an entry in his table for North Vietnam total attack sorties, which he lists as 304,347, but is actually 304,345.

The 306,318 tactical and B-52 Arc Light sorties against the North constituted less than a third (28.26 percent) of all strike sorties in this period. South Vietnam accounted for slightly over half of all attack sorties (54.80 percent). Laotian trail interdiction attack sorties totaled 183,812 (16.94 percent).

US AND SOUTH VIETNAMESE ATTACK SORTIES OVER NORTH VIETNAM, 1965–68[1,2]							
	USAF	USN	USMC	SAC	RVNAF	Year Total	Percent
1965	11,599	13,783	26	0	614	26,022	08.44
1966	44,482	32,954	3,695	223	814	82,168	26.67
1967	54,316	42,587	8,672	1,364	127	107,066	34.74
1968[3]	41,057	40,848	10,326	686	0	92,917	30.15
Totals	151,454	130,172	22,719	2,273	1,555	308,173	100.00

Notes
1 From Van Staaveren, Toward a Bombing Halt, OAFH 1970, Table 3, p. 70. I have corrected his computed total tactical attack sorties, which he lists as 304,347 but which should be 304,345.
2 From USAF, Southeast Asia Review 1961–1973, MS (C6)m May 6, 1974, p. 32.
3 January–March only. I have corrected his computed total tactical attack sorties for 1968, which should be 92,231, not the 92,233 that he lists, which, when added to the SAC figure, gives the 92,917 listed here.

US airmen flew 304,345 tactical strike sorties: 151,454 Air Force (49.76 percent), 130,172 Navy (42.77 percent), and 22,719 Marine (7.47 percent). SAC flew 2,273 B-52 missions, bringing total American strike sorties to 306,618. From 1965 into 1967 the Republic of Vietnam Air Force flew 1,555 sorties over the North, combined American and RVNAF sorties totaling 308,173.

TARGETS REPORTED DAMAGED OR DESTROYED BY CATEGORY, 1965–1968[1]					
Target Categories		1965[2]	1966	1967	1968[3]
Military	AAA Sites	115	1,187	1,923	930
	SAM Sites	11	127	236	109
	C3 inc. Radar[2]	51	153	140	103
	Bases/Airfields/Other	13	8	807	307
Petroleum–Oil–Lubricants	Facilities and Tankage	6	?[4]	140	915
Logistics & Infrastructure	Factories, Buildings, and Warehouses	4,885	9,159	5,093	2,292
	Locks and Dams	9	?[4]	?[4]	?[4]
	Power Plants	5	?[4]	39	6
Transportation	Trail and Road Cuts	847	7,928	6,485	5,813
	Bridges, Ports, Yards, & Ferry Slips	993	4,076	844	(3,099)[5]
	Railroad Yards and Rail Cuts	92	847	169	(1,464)[6]
	Road Cuts, Land, & Water Vehicles	5,557	11,056	17,274	13,492
	Rail Vehicles inc. Locomotives	1,290	1,936	2,507	383
Targets Reported Damaged or Destroyed per Year	Total by Year	1965	1966	1967	1968
	Military	190	1,475	3,106	1,449
	Petroleum-Oil-Lubricants	6	?[4]	140	915
	Logistics/Infrastructure	4,899	9,159[4]	5,132[4]	2,298[4]
	Transportation	8,779	25,843[4]	26,519[4]	(24,251)[5,6]
Targets Damaged or Destroyed per Year (Total 114,161)[4]		13,874	36,477[4]	34,897[4]	28,913[4]
US Joint Service Attack Sorties over DRV (Total 304,345)		25,408	81,131	105,575	92,231
US Aircraft Losses to DRV Air Defenses (Total 881)[7]		163	280	329	109
Targets Damaged or Destroyed per Aircraft Lost		85.12	130.28	106.07	265.26
Strike Sorties Accomplished per Aircraft Lost		155.88	289.75	320.90	846.16
Aircraft Loss Rate per 1,000 Sorties		6.42	3.45	3.12	1.18

Notes

1 Computed from raw data from Melyan and Bonetti, Rolling Thunder Jul 1965–Dec 1966 (PACAF CHECO, 15 Jul 1967), Overton, Rolling Thunder Jan 1967–Nov 1968 (PACAF CHECO, 1 Oct. 1969), Figs 5 & 6; and from White, Rolling Thunder to Linebacker (USACGSC, MA Thesis, 2014).

2 Data from July 1965 onwards.

3 Data through September 1968.

4 Data incomplete and/or provisional summation.

5 Correll, The AF in the Vietnam War (AF Association, 2004), p. 18; total bridges destroyed or damaged during *Rolling Thunder*.

6 Correll, The AF in the Vietnam War, p. 18; total railroad cuts over all *Rolling Thunder*.

7 Where sources differ (for example, losses for 1967 are 321, 328, and 329 depending on source), the author has chosen what seems the more accurate figure.

The table above presents attacks against four target sets: military facilities (air defense radars, airfields, SAM and AAA sites, command and control, and bases and facilities); petroleum–oil–lubricants (POL, storage tanks and distribution facilities), logistics and infrastructure (factories, buildings, warehouses, locks and dams, and power plants); and transportation (bridges, ports, ferry slips, highways/roads/trails, railyards, railroads, and road, rail, and water traffic). Allowing for differing sources, American and South Vietnamese airmen expended approximately 643,000 tons of bombs, rockets, and other ordnance on roughly 115,000 targets. On average, transportation attacks accounted for about 75 percent, logistics attacks about 19 percent, military facility attacks about 5 percent, and POL attacks a little less than 1 percent.

Rolling Thunder cost 881 aircraft lost "Up North," almost 24 per month (the ADF-VPAF claimed 1,331, "572 of which crashed on the spot"). Losses jumped from 163 in 1965, to 280 in 1966, 329 in 1967, and finally 109 in 1968. Approximately 475 were Air Force, 382 Navy, and the remaining two dozen Marine. SA-2s shot down 112 aircraft; MiGs shot down 50. Heavy, medium, light, and small arms fire claimed most of the remaining 719, confirming the

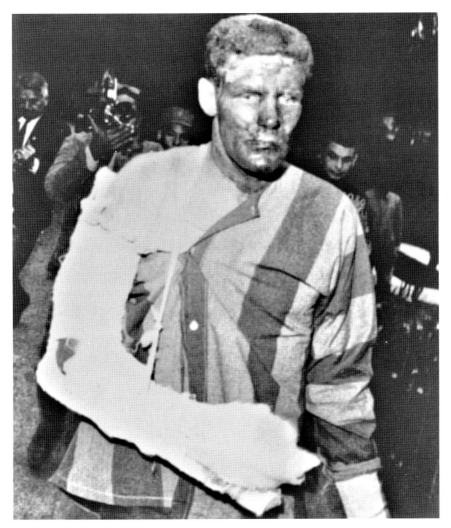

Though badly injured ejecting from his tumbling McDonnell F-4B Phantom II (BuNo 151014) after flak over Kép on December 2, 1966 blew off its left wing, radar intercept officer (RIO) Ensign David G. Rehmann of VF-154 was nevertheless forced by his captors to walk past gawking cameramen, beginning a brutal captivity of over six years. His pilot, Lieutenant (jg) David E. McRae, perished in the shoot-down. (NHHC)

traditional lethality of conventional antiaircraft fire. In the worst year, 1965, the strike aircraft loss rate was 6.42 aircraft lost per 1,000 sorties. In 1967, *Rolling Thunder*'s peak year, the United States lost 329 aircraft (188 USAF, 129 USN, and 12 USMC). That year SA-2s destroyed 62; MiGs 25; heavy, medium, light, and small-arms fire 205; breakdown and pilot error 32, and five simply disappeared. Averaging $1.43 million US apiece in then-year dollars, the 881 aircraft lost over the North totaled $1.26 billion US, equivalent to $9.36 billion US in 2017 (£7.25 billion UK, or €7.94 billion).

Over *Rolling Thunder*, 413 USAF, 92 USMC, and 83 USN aircrew perished, 1.61 percent of the 36,540 American SEA deaths from 1965 through 1968. Many perished in accidents, including 178 sailors and airmen killed in two devastating fires aboard *Oriskany* and *Forrestal*. For those individuals actually hit in combat, the air warfare ratio of killed to wounded has always been higher than land warfare, where, traditionally, wounded greatly exceed killed. In Vietnam, two airmen died for every wounded airman: by comparison, one Army soldier died for every three soldiers wounded, and one Marine died for every eight Marines wounded.

On average, 40 percent of aircrew shot down over the North perished. Of those that survived, little over half (53 percent) were rescued, the rest taken POW or remaining Missing in Action. Over *Rolling Thunder*, naval and Air Force combat search and rescue (CSAR) forces completed 276 combat rescues, over 68 under fire; 95 other attempts failed for various reasons. These "saves" came at the price of 45 aircraft lost, the deaths of over 50 aircrew, and the capture of ten others.

PAVN losses are less clear. A compilation by Roger Boniface of VPAF aircrew killed during *Rolling Thunder* identified 109, to which could be added the 14 North Koreans. On the ground, hundreds, and likely thousands, of SAM and antiaircraft crews perished, undoubtedly including some Chinese and Soviet military personnel, and perhaps others of the various Communist Bloc nations. Civilian deaths are uncertain; one estimate claims approximately 50,000. The DRV acknowledges suffering over one million military dead during the entire Vietnam War; South Vietnam's military lost approximately 250,000 killed over the same period.

Rolling Thunder in retrospect

To some, *Rolling Thunder* represents wasted effort. To others, it constitutes a textbook study in the limitations inherent to air power. For many airmen, it reflects not the *limits* of air power, but rather *limitations imposed upon* air power. In truth, it blended all of these: poorly planned, with vague and ill-defined goals, plagued by politically induced limitations and outright meddling, sporadic in execution, and undertaken in the last years of the unguided

The contrast with Linebacker I/II

In 1972, the PAVN invaded the South with over 100,000 troops in 14 divisions and 26 regiments, with 600 tanks, heavy artillery, and portable SA-7 SAMs. American air power forces in theater were less than half what they had been at the height of *Rolling Thunder*. Available Air Force tactical strike, reconnaissance, Weasel, and electronic warfare airplanes had dropped from 710 in 1968 to 329 in 1972 and Navy carriers from six in 1968 to two in early 1972, while Marine air was back in Japan. President Richard Nixon, Secretary of Defense Melvin Laird, and Joint Chiefs Chairman Admiral Thomas Moorer ordered forces strengthened in SEA, the Navy sending four carriers, the Marines deploying fighter, attack, and electronic warfare squadrons, and the Air Force nearly doubling its fighter, attack, and bomber strength. Joined with ground resistance, this force, in 38,032 sorties (24,079 USAF, 10,098 USN, and 3,855 USMC) employing new precision weapons, halted the PAVN in bloody defeat, saving the South.

In December 1972, faced with continued DRV intransigence at the Paris peace talks, President Richard M. Nixon ordered a resumption of bombing over the North, his key staff influenced by a think-piece prepared in October by a small six-person team led by Air Force Colonel (later Major General) Richard V. Secord. Secord's team proposed (as he recalled) "an all-out aerial assault on the North, utilizing our B-52s for the first time, and striking military targets which had previously been off limits for various reasons." In mid-December Secord was told "the paper should be dusted off as we were going to war." Influenced by a book he had recently read on Eighth Air Force operations against Germany, he drafted a strike order, stressing "maximum effort." On December 17, the JCS issued an execute message using those words.

Called *Linebacker II*, the resulting campaign lasted from December 18–29, pausing for Christmas. Over 11 days, B-52s executed 729 night sorties, hitting 34 targets and dropping 15,000 tons of bombs. In their cells, POWs awoke to the shriek of falling bombs and the flash of thunderous explosions. "Gasps of fright, awe, terror and despair slipped from the mouths of guards," Colonel George "Bud" Day recalled; "Vietnamese who had claimed that they had defeated US air power now came to understand that they had never seen air power." At month's end, the DRV went back to the talks. "Prior to *Linebacker II*, the North Vietnamese were intransigent, buying time, refusing even to discuss a formal meeting schedule," one delegate stated; "After *Linebacker II*, they were shaken, demoralized, [and] anxious to talk about anything." Success came at the price of 15 B-52s lost, from questionable tactics negating jamming and leaving them vulnerable to SA-2s, particularly during turns. *Linebacker II* cost 27 aircraft, 43 aircrew killed or missing, 41 captured, and 33 recovered. On January 21, 1973, a ceasefire took effect; on January 27, both parties signed the Peace Accords; and on February 12, Operation *Homecoming* began flying ex-POWs from Hanoi's Gia Lam airfield.

For a while it seemed South Vietnam might go the way of South Korea after July 1953. But then came Watergate. "When Nixon stepped down because of Watergate we knew we would win," Colonel Bui Tin told journalist Stephen Young; "We tested [President Gerald] Ford's resolve by attacking Phuoc Long in January 1975. When Ford kept American B-52s in their hangars, our leadership decided on a big offensive against South Vietnam." In 1975, PAVN tanks overran the South in only six weeks, bringing the war to a tragic and bitter close.

"dumb" bomb, it could hardly have succeeded as badly structured and executed as it was. Over time, the airmen compensated for these deficiencies by simply becoming very, very good at what they did. For example, in 1968, attacks on supply lines north of the Song Lam (Lam river) in Nghe An province seriously impeded shipments south to Ha Tinh, the PAVN reporting that "supplies and weapons piled up at chokepoints," with monthly shipping rates dropping from 6,500 tons in April to just over 1,400 tons in June. Ironically, reducing attacks over the North worked more to solve the PAVN's problem than any organizational and other changes that they made.

The Vietnam morass reflected flawed decision-making at many levels, from the grand strategic to the tactical. The first stemmed from Harry Truman's inconsistent post-1945 Far East policy. While wisely opposing continued British and Dutch rule over India and the East Indies, he acceded in May 1950 to French pleas for military aid for Indochina. By mid-1954, American taxpayers were funding nearly 80 percent of its Indochina war, with hundreds of military and CIA contract personnel serving in-country. Without American support, France would have had to negotiate a withdrawal before 1950. Such an early transition might have enabled indigenous anti-Communist Vietnamese to frustrate the ambitions of Ho Chi Minh, Le Duan, and other Vietnamese Marxists, as they were then far from supreme in securing their dominance and control of Vietnam's anticolonialist movement.

Next was the Kennedy administration's ill-considered support of Laotian neutralization in July 1962. Laos constituted the strategic ground in Southeast Asia, and the accords worked only in the DRV's favor, enabling expansion of the Ho Chi Minh Trail bypassing the DMZ. Within a year, South Vietnam's insurgency exploded into full fury.

The third mistake was the overthrow and murder of Ngo Dinh Diem. Whatever flaws Diem possessed, he was a patriot, opposed to the corruption and factionalism that, after his death, categorized South Vietnam's government. His death exposed the chronic careerism of South Vietnam's generals, too many of whom were fixated upon advancing their own power, and the Kennedy administration's sad complicity tarnished America's presence with brush-strokes of expediency and inept Machiavellianism.

Then comes *Rolling Thunder*, which teaches:

- campaign planning is best left to military professionals, not politicians
- nothing substitutes for a coherent and focused campaign plan
- military loyalty must extend down the chain of command as well as up and
- politicians should not frivolously send military forces into combat (and certainly not – viz. Johnson's and Richard Russell's anguished telephone calls in March 1965 – when they see neither hope nor prospect of success).

In an apt epitaph, Edward Drea wrote, "Lacking an integrated and coherent political-military strategic foundation, the air campaign proceeded by fits and starts, sputtering most of the time."

From its outset, it lacked a decent plan; organizational and institutional cohesiveness; rootedness in sound strategy; and clear chain of command. It mixed distant political intervention with fragmented theater-level direction, and untrusting suspicion between the administration's military and civilian leaders. (McNamara recalled, "My civilian staff and I would receive the recommendations from the Chiefs, examine them, and then submit separate recommendations to the President. Invariably my recommendations were for lesser bombing than recommended by the Chiefs.") Though airmen, at great risk and loss, struck many targets, there were few lasting effects. Statistics of destroyed vehicles, cut roads, and blasted buildings steadily rose, but meant little, for, with rare exception, Hanoi retained the ability to prosecute its war.

Operation *Homecoming*: newly freed former prisoners of war cheer as their Lockheed C-141A Starlifter (SN 66-0177) departs Gia Lam airport on February 12, 1973. Named *Hanoi Taxi* and later rebuilt as a stretched C-141C, this Starlifter is now exhibited at the National Museum of the USAF. (NMUSAF)

Only McNamara's decision not to attack SAM sites under construction in April–July 1965 exceeded his folly in placing MiG bases off-limits until mid-1967. Both decisions cost airmen's lives and freedom. The synergy of MiGs, SAMs, and AAA worked to sharply ramp up losses, diverting thousands of sorties from campaign objectives towards air defense suppression.

Lack of clearly defined command and control led to confusion and duplication of air effort, and an interservice battle over managing air power. No single figure possessed authority, responsibility, span of control, and freedom of action comparable to that which General Charles Horner exercised as Joint and Combined Force Air Component Commander (JFACC/CFACC) during *Desert Storm*.

In 1975, Robert McNamara told Walt Rostow, "The Joint Chiefs of Staff laid out a target system in North Vietnam to maximize the damage to North Vietnam." But the Joint Chiefs' 94-target list, for all its merits, constituted neither a "target system," nor a "plan," nor even the outline of a plan. What was never furnished was an outcome-oriented effects-based campaign plan. As former senior staff officer Colonel Bui Tin stated in 1995, "If all the bombing had been concentrated at one time, it would have hurt our efforts. But the bombing was expanded in slow stages under Johnson and it didn't worry us. We had plenty of time to prepare alternative routes and facilities."

The PAVN rapidly rebuilt damaged infrastructure and restored services lost to *Rolling Thunder*. In January 1969, Air Force intelligence concluded that the DRV "had returned to almost normal economic activity. The volume of supplies moving south had almost doubled." PACOM intelligence concluded, "The North Vietnamese presently have complete freedom of movement south to the DMZ and west to the Laos border. Rail service is continuous to

Vinh. Bridges that have not been used regularly since the bombing started are up and in use on LOCs [lines of communications] leading to the DMZ. In short, the logistic machinery is now functioning without restraint at levels never reached at any time, even before the war."

Increasingly large antiwar demonstrations worked against continued bombing. "[They were] essential to our strategy," Colonel Bui Tin recalled; "Every day our leadership would listen to world news over the radio at 9 a.m. to follow the growth of the American antiwar movement. Visits to Hanoi by people like Jane Fonda, and former Attorney General Ramsey Clark and ministers gave us confidence that we should hold on in the face of battlefield reverses. We were elated when Jane Fonda, wearing a red Vietnamese dress, said at a press conference that she was ashamed of American actions in the war and that she would struggle along with us."

The military legacy

Rolling Thunder triggered widespread changes that reshaped Western air power in time for the last decade of the Cold War. An air-to-air missile study overseen by Navy Captain Frank Ault expanded to examine training, leading to Miramar's Top Gun program, and the joint-service AIMVAL–ACEVAL evaluation that reshaped air-to-air combat and missile development and testing. *Rolling Thunder* MiG-killer Colonel William Kirk and Majors Larry Keith and Richard "Moody" Suter transformed Nellis' Weapons School, making it less formulaic and dogmatic and emphasizing careful instruction to produce the best possible graduates. Suter's work led to Red Flag, the strike package exercises that generated *Desert Storm*'s success. Accompanying these were new instrumented threat ranges, fighters – the F-14, F-15, F-16, and F/A-18 – that were more than nuclear strike aircraft masquerading under the fighter name, and more useful weapons tested to wartime, not peacetime, standards.

The dangers inherent in confronting heavily redundant, layered, and highly integrated air defense networks, highlighted again in 1973 during the costly October Arab–Israeli War, forced investment in electronic combat, including jammers, new anti-radar missiles like the AGM-88 HARM and British ALARM, and "stealth."

Rolling Thunder ended just months before the first combat use of Paveway laser-guided bombs (LGB), which changed air power from the "number of sorties required to destroy a target" to the "number of targets destroyed per sortie." Coupled with infrared sensors that turned night to day, the LGB ensured that future wars would be vastly different than those that preceded them.

Rolling Thunder through the eyes of its airmen

Vietnam is vastly different than a half-century ago, and would be unrecognizable to Ho Chi Minh and Le Duan, having evolved from a hard-line Communist state seeking to rival the PRC and USSR as a spreader of global revolution, into a market-driven (if still authoritarian) one well-integrated into the regional Association of Southeast Asian Nations (ASEAN). With societal change came as well a change in its diplomatic relations with the United States, evident by growing trade, educational exchanges, and even military cooperation between the two nations.

Happily, as relations between Vietnam and America have improved, airmen – like other veterans of that war – have begun their own reconciliations. In 2000, a group of Misty F-100F pilots met former PAVN veterans who had shot at them and run supplies down the Trail, finding ties of mutual if guarded respect. In April 2016, 11 American fighter pilots met in Hanoi with former VPAF opponents. What began cautiously ended in collegiality, and resulted in a dozen aging MiG pilots meeting a larger group of Americans in San Diego in September 2017. "American pilots were ordered there, sent to defend their country," said

BELOW THE SHAPE OF ATTACKS TO COME

This illustration shows the basic Paveway LGB delivery tactic in the early 1970s. The LGB transformed attacks on pinpoint targets when it was introduced, a few months after Rolling Thunder ended.

1. Both Phantoms are at 18,000ft above ground level. Bomber F-4D (red) is moving faster than Illuminator F-4D (orange), whose back-seater (Weapons System Officer) is searching for the target. Bomber is at Mach 0.85, Illuminator is at Mach 0.78. Illuminator remains at 18,000ft throughout the attack.
2. Bomber pulls a hard descending turn to drop after hearing the Illuminator call that the target has been "spotlighted" by the laser.
3. Bomber is at 15,000ft and diving in about a 30-degree dive, and Mach 0.9.
4. Bomber drops Paveway bomb at 12,000ft and begins immediate pull-up and afterburner climb.
5. Bomber is at 15,000ft and climbing, begins turn to rejoin with Illuminator. Bomb, following Illuminator's laser, hits target and explodes.
6. Bomber rejoining with Illuminator at 18,000ft.
7. Bomber and Illuminator are both in level flight exiting target area at Mach 0.95.

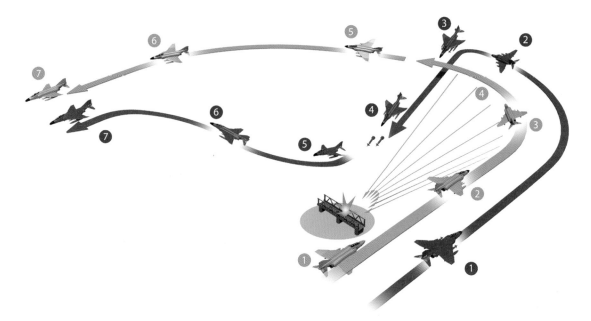

retired Senior Colonel Nguyen Van Bay, an 82-year-old former 923rd Regiment MiG-17F pilot, adding "If we didn't shoot them, they'd shoot us. We were doing our jobs. That's the past. Now we're friends."

But if passions toward former foes have cooled, *Rolling Thunder*'s airmen remain bitter toward Lyndon Johnson and Robert McNamara. The Mistys who visited Vietnam in 2000 spent their last night at a bittersweet dinner at Saigon's Rex Hotel. "The war, they all believed, was poorly planned and badly managed," Rick Newman and Don Shepperd reported, "and they were still angry. Not at the communists, but at their own leaders, especially Robert McNamara and Lyndon Johnson and the Congress that cut off an ally in the middle of a war."

"President Johnson was serious when he said that we couldn't even hit an outhouse without his permission," Colonel Jacksel "Jack" Broughton, the charismatic former Vice Commander of the 355th TFW wrote after the war. "He and McNamara lost a bunch of good people and good machinery all over Southeast Asia with their outhouse mentality."

On June 1, 2015, 50 years after the beginning of *Rolling Thunder*, the United States and Vietnam executed a joint vision statement on regional defense, signed by then-US Secretary of Defense Ash Carter (left) and then-Vietnamese Defense Minister General Phung Quang Thanh, who as a young soldier had fought with the PAVN. (DoD)

"We could not understand our country's lack of direction," Colonel Bud Day, one of America's most heroic POWs, wrote; "The indecisiveness only encouraged the Vietnamese to greater efforts. The timid bombing policies, the piecemeal attacks, the misuse of US air power, only resulted in squandering the lives of pilots, destruction of high-priced aircraft, and the waste of young American blood on the battlefields of Vietnam."

"We were really unhappy about how that war was conducted," Lieutenant General Michael Short, a Vietnam F-4C pilot, recalled in 2001, adding, "We bitched about it in the bar at night and got drunk, but we sobered up and went flying the next day. We were as good as we could be."

"All of us in *Desert Storm* had memories of Vietnam and we were determined not to repeat the mistakes of that war," General Charles Horner, a Wild Weasel who commanded coalition air forces in *Desert Storm*, reminisced; "I would accept information and advice from any source, but I maintained strict control of targeting."

"So what did *Rolling Thunder* accomplish? Not so much," A-4 pilot Vice Admiral Robert F. Dunn recalled in 2015, adding, "A lot of ordnance was expended, vast quantities of materials of various sorts were used up, and hundreds of aircraft were lost to both operational accidents and combat. Air Force and naval aviators lost their lives by the score, and hundreds more became prisoners in Hanoi… May the politicians and leadership of the future do better."

Admiral Dunn's admonition rightly reflects a continuing challenge. For airmen, *Rolling Thunder* is shorthand for "How Not To" plan and execute an air campaign, but it means little to politicians. In 1999, the politically micro-managed Operation *Allied Force* over the former Yugoslavia mirrored *Rolling Thunder*'s gradualism and timidity, endangering the alliance itself until NATO military leaders forcefully emphasized the need for a more focused and sustained campaign. *Rolling Thunder*-like gradualism and political hesitancy, with obsessive concern over casualty counts, has characterized recent air operations over Libya, Iraq, and Syria. Clearly, learning from *Rolling Thunder* remains relevant not merely for airmen, but also for politicians, even in this era of smart bombs, satellite-cued weapons, cyber warfare, and killer drones.

FURTHER READING

Anderegg, C. R., *Sierra Hotel* (USAF History and Museums Program, 2001)

Barker, Patrick, "The SA-2 and Wild Weasel: The Nature of Technological Change in Military Systems," M.A. Thesis (Lehigh University, 1994)

Basel, Gene I., *Pak Six* (Jove, 1987)

Bell, Ken, *100 Missions North* (Potomac Books, 1993)

Berger, Carl, et al., *The United States Air Force in Southeast Asia* (USAF Office of AF History, 1977)

Boniface, Roger, *MiGs over North Vietnam* (Stackpole, 2010)

Broughton, Jack, *Thud Ridge* (Lippincott, 1969)

Broughton, Jack, *Going Downtown* (Orion, 1988)

Cagle, Malcom W, "Task Force 77 in Action off Vietnam," *Naval Institute Proceedings* 98, no. 831 (May 1972): 66–109

Clodfelter, Mark, *The Limits of Air Power* (Free Press, 1989)

Congress, U.S., Senate, *Air War against North Vietnam: Hearings before the Preparedness Investigating Subcommittee of Committee on Armed Services,* Part 2, August 1967 (Government Printing Office, 1967)

Corum, Delbert, et al. and Paul Burbage, ed. by A. J. C. Lavalle, *The Tale of Two Bridges* and *The Battle for the Skies over North Vietnam* (USAF Air University, 1976)

Courtois, Stéphane, et al., *The Black Book of Communism* (Harvard, 1999)

Cunningham, Case A., "William W. Momyer: A Biography of an Airpower Mind," Ph.D. Dissertation (USAF School of Advanced Air and Space Studies, 2013)

Day, George E., *Return with Honor* (Champlin Museum Press, 1989)

Denton, Jeremiah A., Jr, with A. I. Brandt, *When Hell was in Session* (Readers Digest Press, 1976)

Dobrynin, Anatoly, *In Confidence* (Times Books, 1995)

Drea, Edward J., *McNamara, Clifford, and the Burdens of Vietnam, 1965–1969* (Secretary of Defense Historical Office, 2011)

Drury, Richard S., *My Secret War* (Aero Publishers, 1979)

Fall, Bernard B., *Street without Joy* (Stackpole, 1961)

Frankum, Ronald B., Jr, *Like Rolling Thunder* (Rowman & Littlefield, 2005)

Fry, Joseph A., *Debating Vietnam* (Rowman & Littlefield, 2006)

Futrell, Robert Frank, et al., *Aces and Aerial Victories* (USAF Air University, 1976)

Futrell, Robert Frank, with Martin Blumenson, *The USAF in Southeast Asia: The Advisory Years to 1965* (USAF Office of AF History, 1981)

Futrell, Robert Frank, *Ideas, Concepts, Doctrine* (USAF Air University, 1989)

Gaiduk, Ilya V., *The Soviet Union and the Vietnam War* (Ivan Dee, 1996)

Galdorisi, George and Tom Phillips, *Leave No Man Behind* (Zenith, 2008)

Goldstein, Gordon M., *Lessons in Disaster* (Times Books, 2008)

Grant, Zalin, *Over the Beach* (Norton, 1986)

Gray, Stephen R., *Rampant Raider* (Naval Institute, 2007)

Grossnick, Roy A. et al., *US Naval Aviation, 1910–1995* (USN Historical Center, 1996)

Guan, Ang Cheng, *The Vietnam War from the Other Side* (RoutledgeCurzon, 2002)

Hampton, Dan, *The Hunter Killers* (Morrow, 2015)

Hobson, Chris, *Vietnam Air Losses: United States Air Force, Navy and Marine Corps Fixed Wing Aircraft Losses in SEA 1961–1973* (Midland, 2001)

Kamps, Charles Tustin, "The JCS 94-Target List: A Vietnam Myth That Still Distorts Military. Thought," *Aerospace Power Journal* 14, no. 1 (Spring 2001): 67–80

Johnson, Lyndon, ed. by Michael Beschloss, *Taking Charge: The Johnson White House Tapes, 1963–1964* (Simon & Schuster, 1997)

Johnson, Lyndon, ed. by Michael Beschloss, *Reaching for Glory: Lyndon Johnson's Secret White House Tapes, 1964–1965* (Simon & Schuster, 2001)

Lane, John J., *Command and Control and Communications Structures in Southeast Asia* (USAF Air University, 1981)

Lewy, Guenter, *America in Vietnam* (Oxford, 1978)

Mahan, Erin R. and Jeffrey A. Larsen, *The Ascendency of the Secretary of Defense* (Secretary of Defense Historical Office, 2013)

Marolda, Edward J. and G. Wesley Price III, *A Short History of the US Navy and the Southeast Asian Conflict* (USN Historical Center, 1984)

Marrett, George J., *Cheating Death* (Smithsonian, 2003)

McCain, John, with Mark Salter, *Faith of my Fathers* (Random House, 1999)

McMaster, H. R., *Dereliction of Duty* (HarperCollins Publishers, 1997)

McNamara, Robert S. with Brian Van De Mark, *In Retrospect* (Times Books, 1995)

Mersky, Peter B. and Norman Polmar, *The Naval Air War in Vietnam* (Nautical and Aviation, 1981)

The "Century Series" c. mid-1950s. Clockwise, from upper right: North American F-100C Super Sabre, McDonnell F-101A Voodoo, Convair F-102A Delta Dagger, Lockheed F-104A Starfighter, Republic YF-105A Thunderchief, and Convair F-106A Delta Dart. (USAF)

Mersky, Peter B., *U.S. Marine Corps Aviation* (Nautical and Aviation, 1983)

Michel, Marshal L., III, *Clashes: Air Combat over North Vietnam, 1965–1972* (Naval Institute, 1997)

Mikesh, Robert C., *Flying Dragons* (Schiffer, 2005)

Momyer, William W., *Air Power in Three Wars* (USAF Air University, 1978)

Moyer, Mark, *Triumph Forsaken* (Cambridge, 2006)

Nichols, John B., with Barrett Tillman. *On Yankee Station* (Naval Institute, 1987)

Nitze, Paul H. with Steven L. Rearden, *From Hiroshima to Glasnost* (Grove Weidenfeld, 1989)

Olds, Robin with Christina Olds and Ed Rasimus, *Fighter Pilot* (St. Martin's, 2010)

Palmer, Bruce, Jr, *The 25-Year War* (University Press of Kentucky, 1984)

Pike, Douglas, *PAVN: People's Army of Vietnam* (Presidio, 1986)

Podhoretz, Norman, *Why We Were in Vietnam* (Simon and Schuster, 1982)

Rasimus, Ed, *When Thunder Rolled* (Ballantine, 2003)

Rearden, Steven L., *Council of War* (U.S. JCS Joint History Office, 2012)

Rochester, Stuart I. and Frederick Kiley, *Honor Bound* (Naval Institute, 1999)

Rusk, Dean and Richard Rusk with Daniel S. Papp, *As I Saw It* (Norton, 1990)

Samuel, Wolfgang, *Glory Days* (Schiffer, 2008)

Schlesinger, Arthur M., Jr, *The Bitter Heritage* (Houghton Mifflin, 1967)

Sharp, U. S. Grant, *Strategy for Defeat* (Presidio, 1978)

Shaw, Geoffrey, *The Lost Mandate of Heaven* (Ignatius, 2015)

Sorley, Lewis, *A Better War* (Harcourt, 1999)

Sorley, Lewis, *Westmoreland* (Houghton Mifflin Harcourt, 2011)

Staaveren, Jacob van, *Gradual Failure* (Air Force History and Museums Program, 2002)

Thompson, James Clay, *Rolling Thunder* (University of North Carolina Press, 1980)

Thompson, Wayne, *To Hanoi and Back* (Smithsonian, 2000)

Thorsness, Leo, *Surviving Hell* (Encounter, 2008)

Tilford, Earl H., Jr, *Setup* (USAF Air University, 1991)

Tilford, Earl H., Jr, *Search and Rescue in Southeast Asia* (USAF Center for Air Force History, 1992)

Tillman, Barrett, *MiG-Master* (Nautical and Aviation, 1980)

Tin, Bui, *Following Ho Chi Minh* (University of Hawaii Press, 1995)

Tin, Bui, *From Enemy to Friend* (Naval Institute, 2002)

Trest, Warren, *Air Force Roles and Missions* (USAF Air University, 1998)

Trotti, John, *Phantom over Vietnam* (Presidio, 1984)

Vick, Alan, *Snakes in the Eagle's Nest* (RAND, 1995)

Werrell, Kenneth P, *Archie, Flak, AAA, and SAM* (USAF Air University, 1988)

Westmoreland, William C., USA, *A Soldier Reports* (Doubleday, 1976)

Winnefeld, James A. and Dana J. Johnson, *Joint Air Operations* (Naval Institute, 1993)

Zhai, Qiang, *China and the Vietnam Wars, 1950–1975* (University of North Carolina Press, 2000)

Zhang, Xiaoming, *Deng Xiaoping's Long War* (University of North Carolina Press, 2015)

INDEX

Page numbers in **bold** refer to figures and those in *italic* refer to tables.